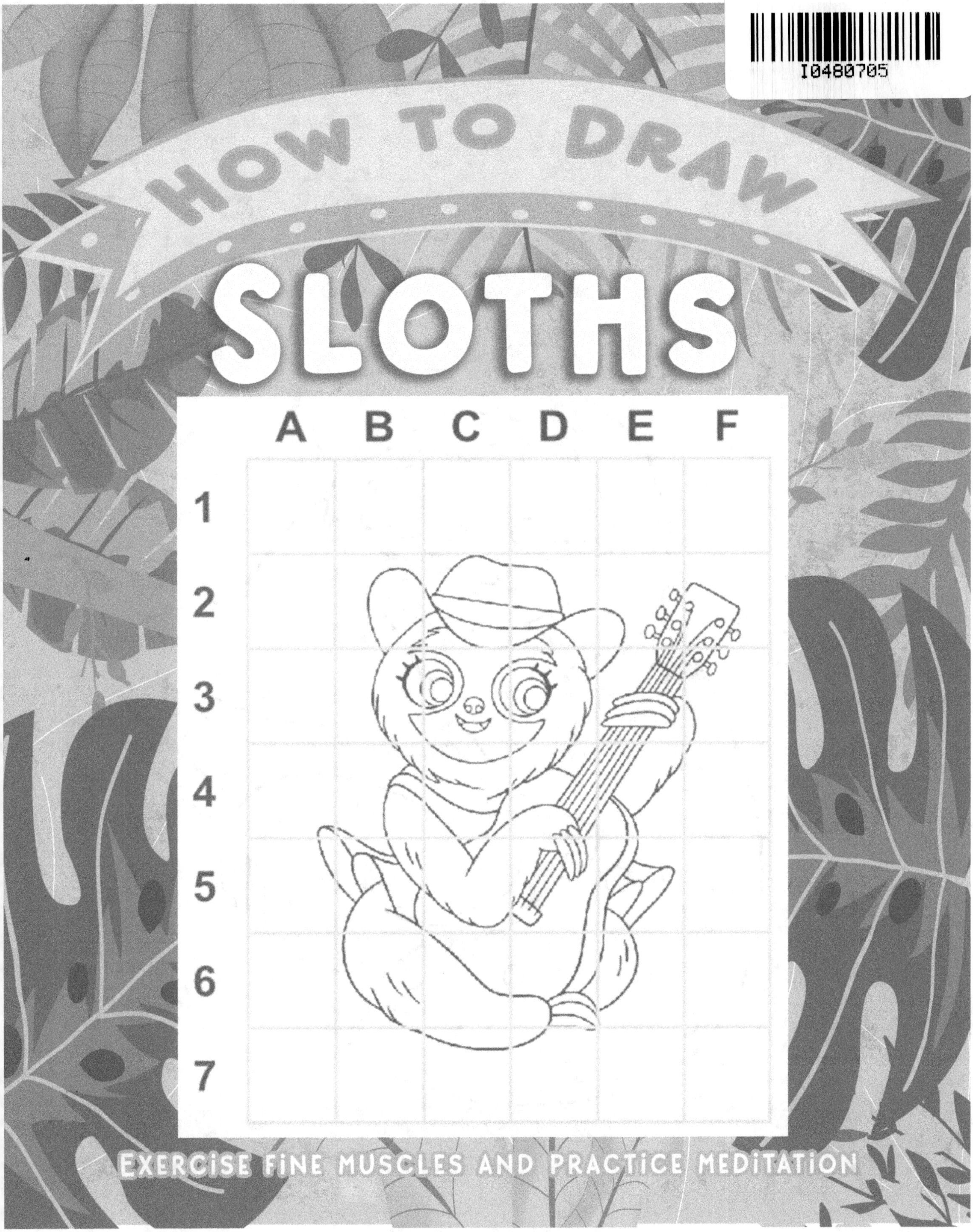
HOW TO DRAW
SLOTHS
A B C D E F
1 2 3 4 5 6 7
EXERCISE FINE MUSCLES AND PRACTICE MEDITATION

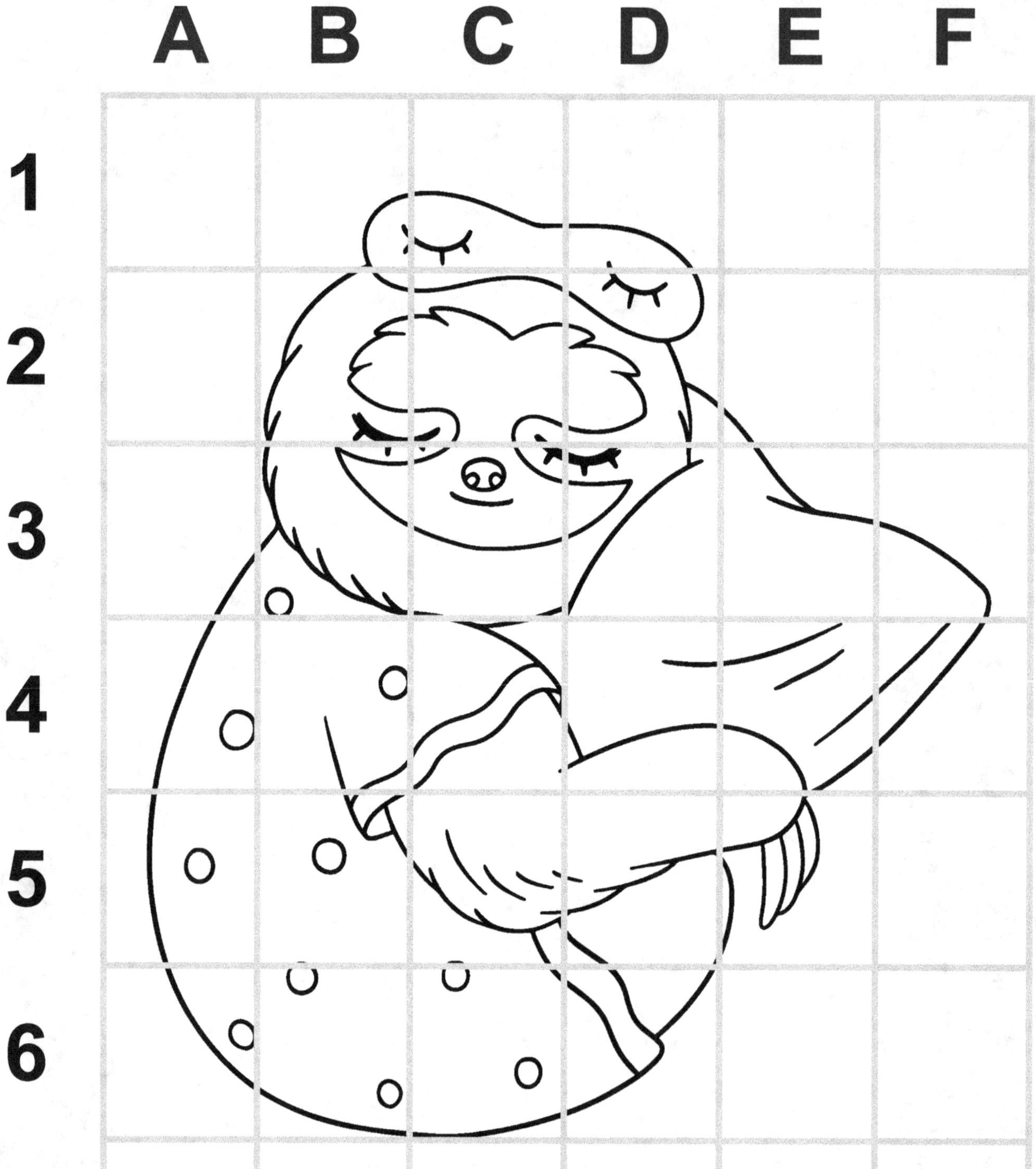
A B C D E F
1
2
3
4
5
6
7

YOUR TURN

	A	B	C	D	E	F
1						
2						
3						
4						
5						
6						
7						

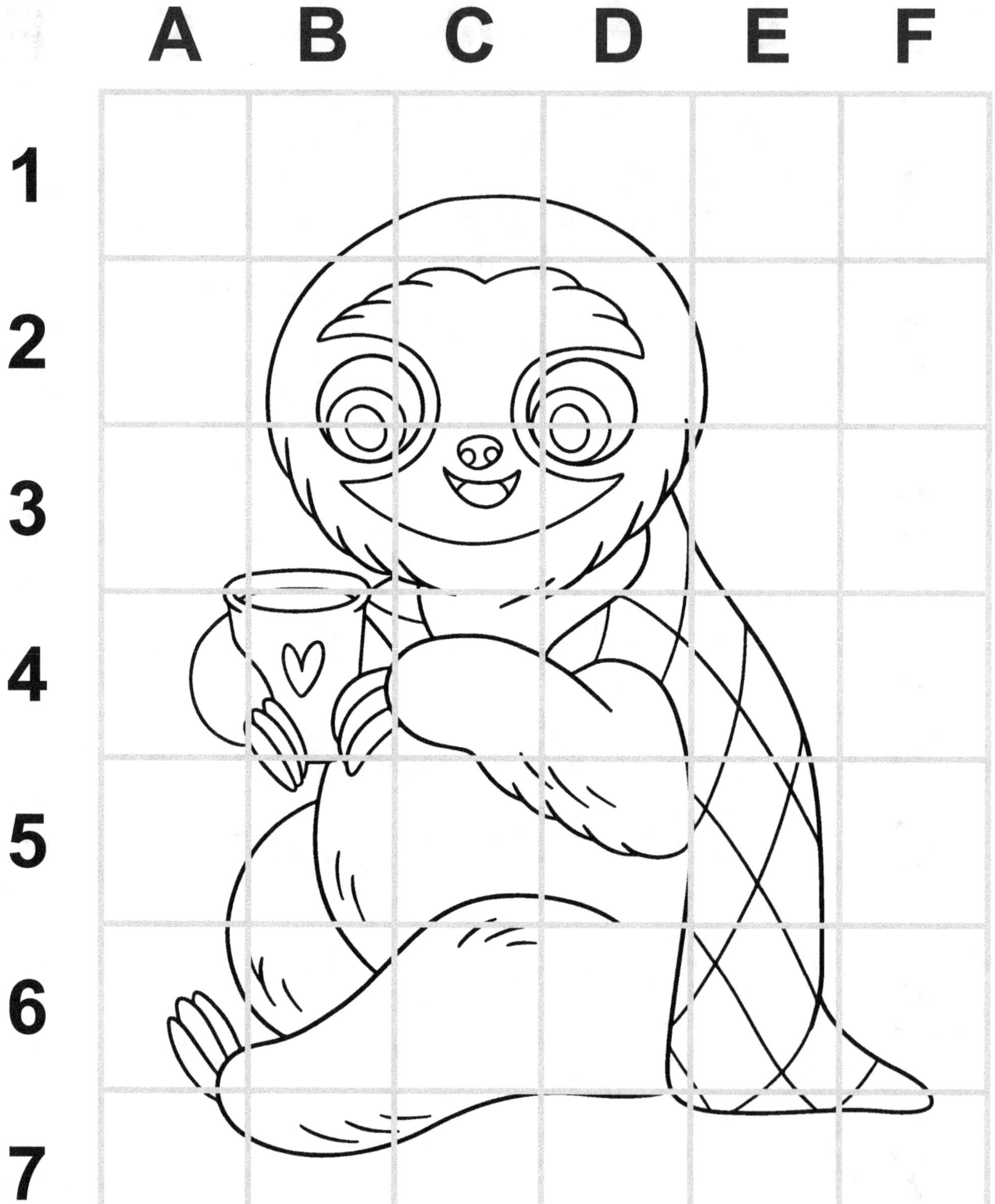

A
B
C
D
E
F
1
2
3
4
5
6
7

YOUR TURN

	A	B	C	D	E	F
1						
2						
3						
4						
5						
6						
7						

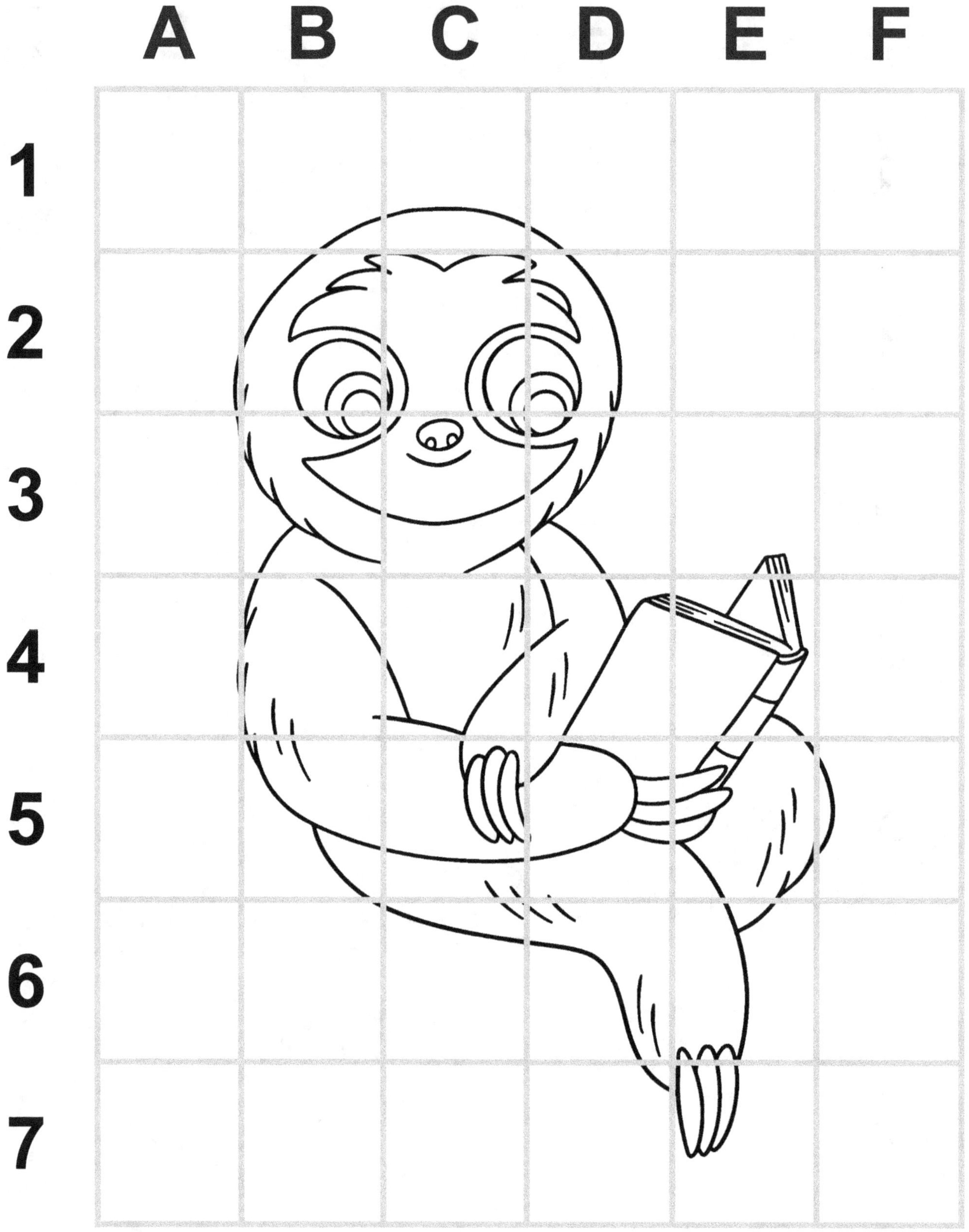
A B C D E F
1
2
3
4
5
6
7

YOUR TURN

	A	B	C	D	E	F
1						
2						
3						
4						
5						
6						
7						

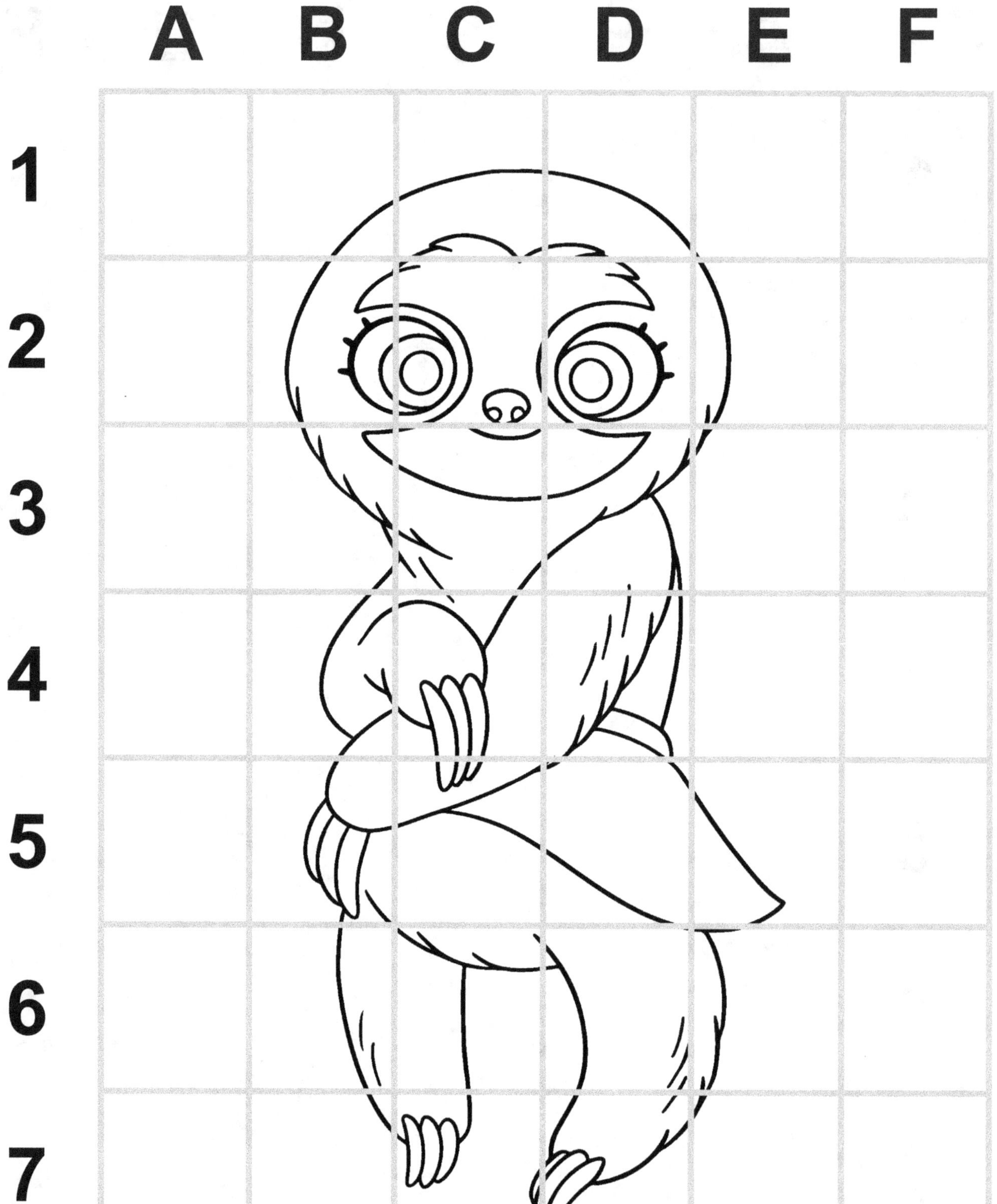
A B C D E F
1
2
3
4
5
6
7

YOUR TURN

	A	B	C	D	E	F
1						
2						
3						
4						
5						
6						
7						

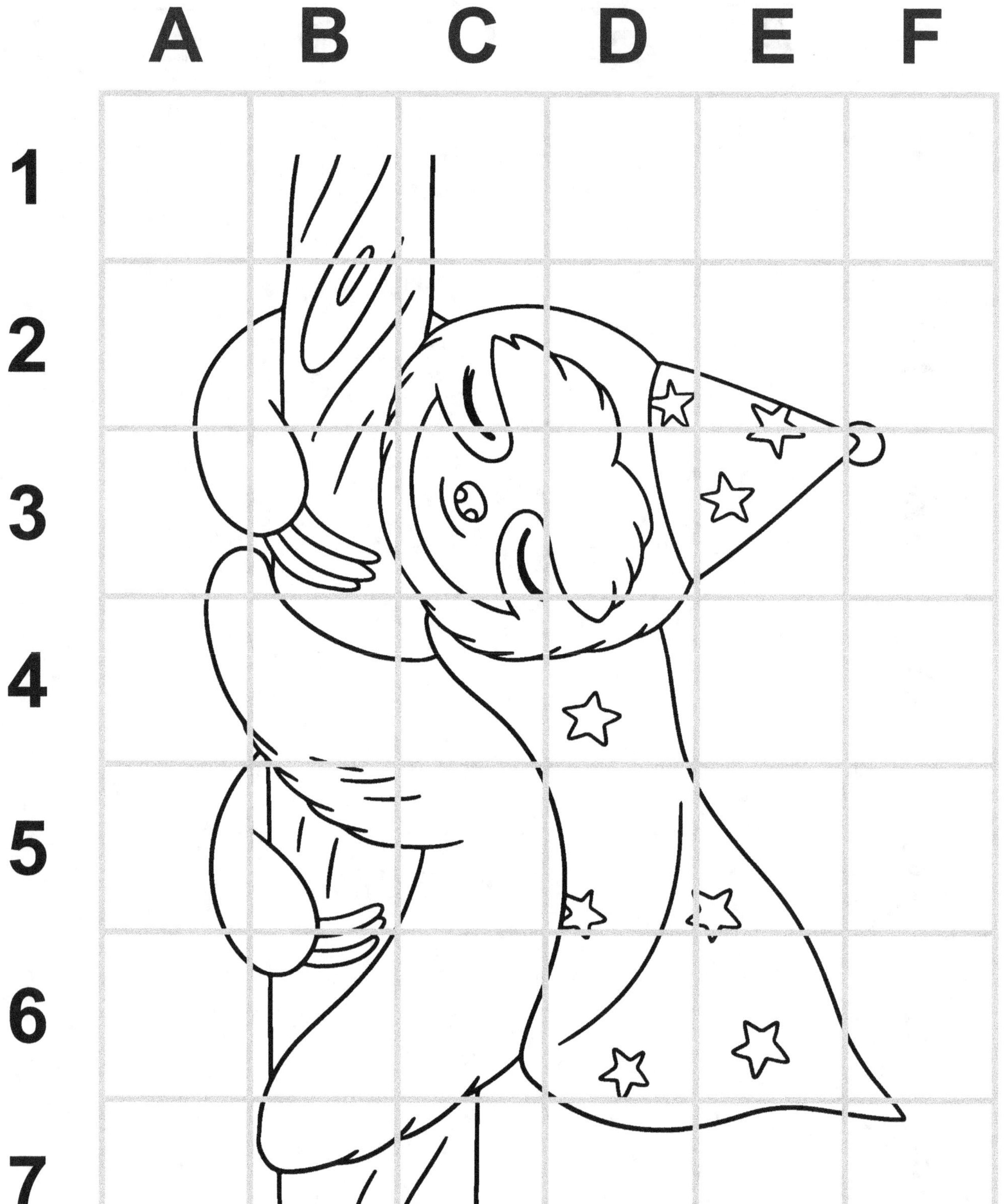
A
B
C
D
E
F
1
2
3
4
5
6
7

YOUR TURN

	A	B	C	D	E	F
1						
2						
3						
4						
5						
6						
7						

A B C D E F

1
2
3
4
5
6
7

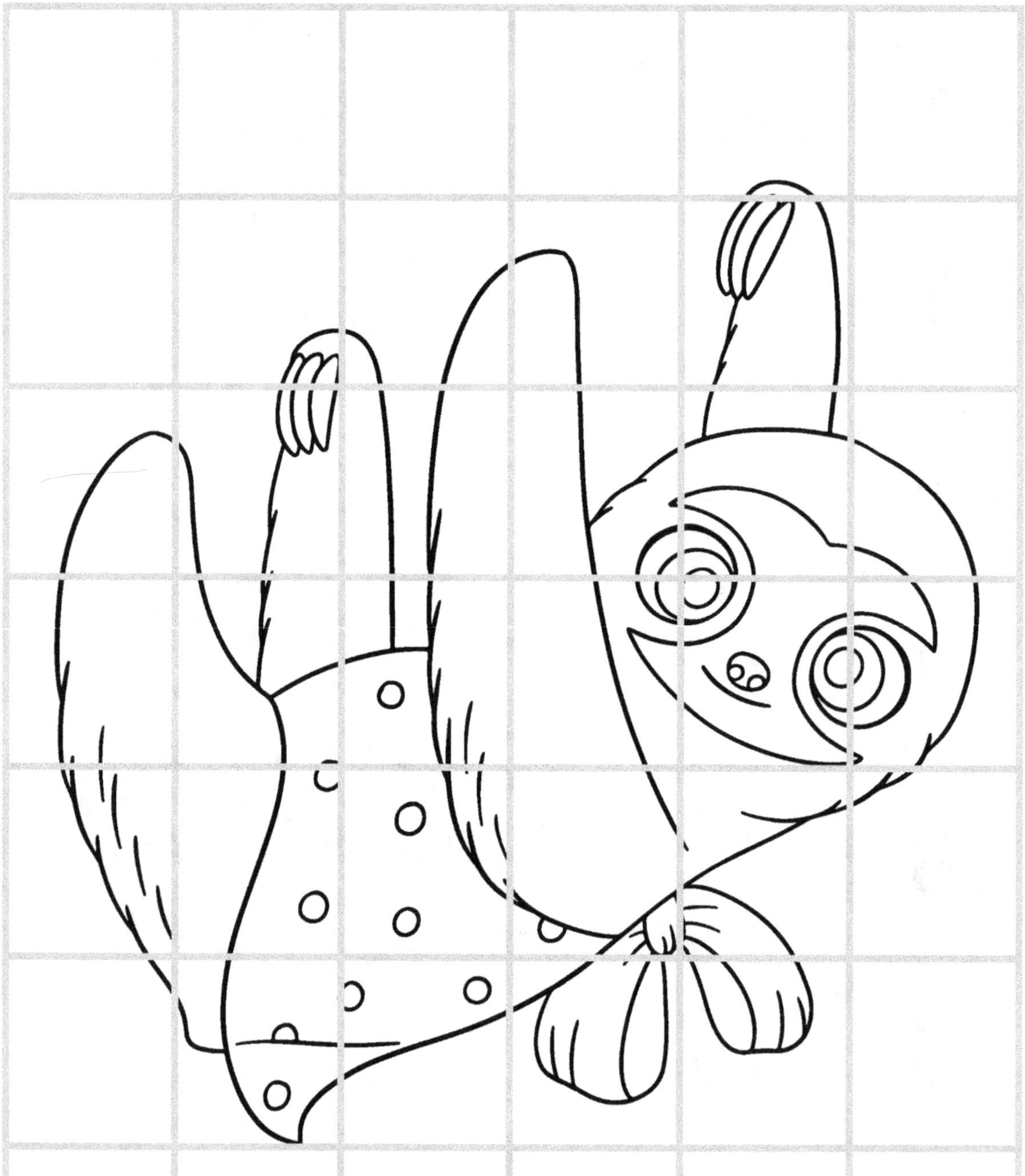

YOUR TURN

	A	B	C	D	E	F
1						
2						
3						
4						
5						
6						
7						

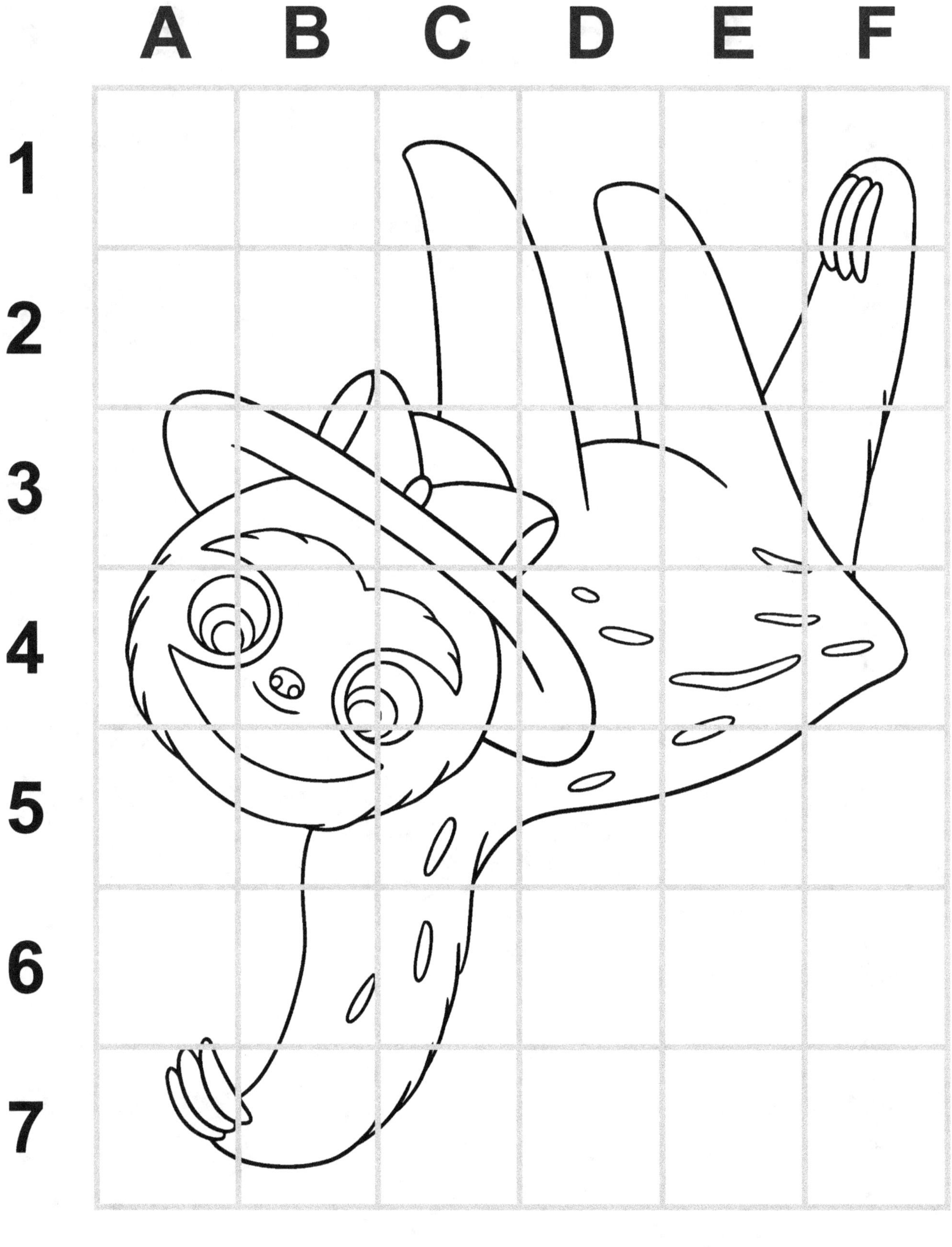
A
B
C
D
E
F
1
2
3
4
5
6
7

YOUR TURN

	A	B	C	D	E	F
1						
2						
3						
4						
5						
6						
7						

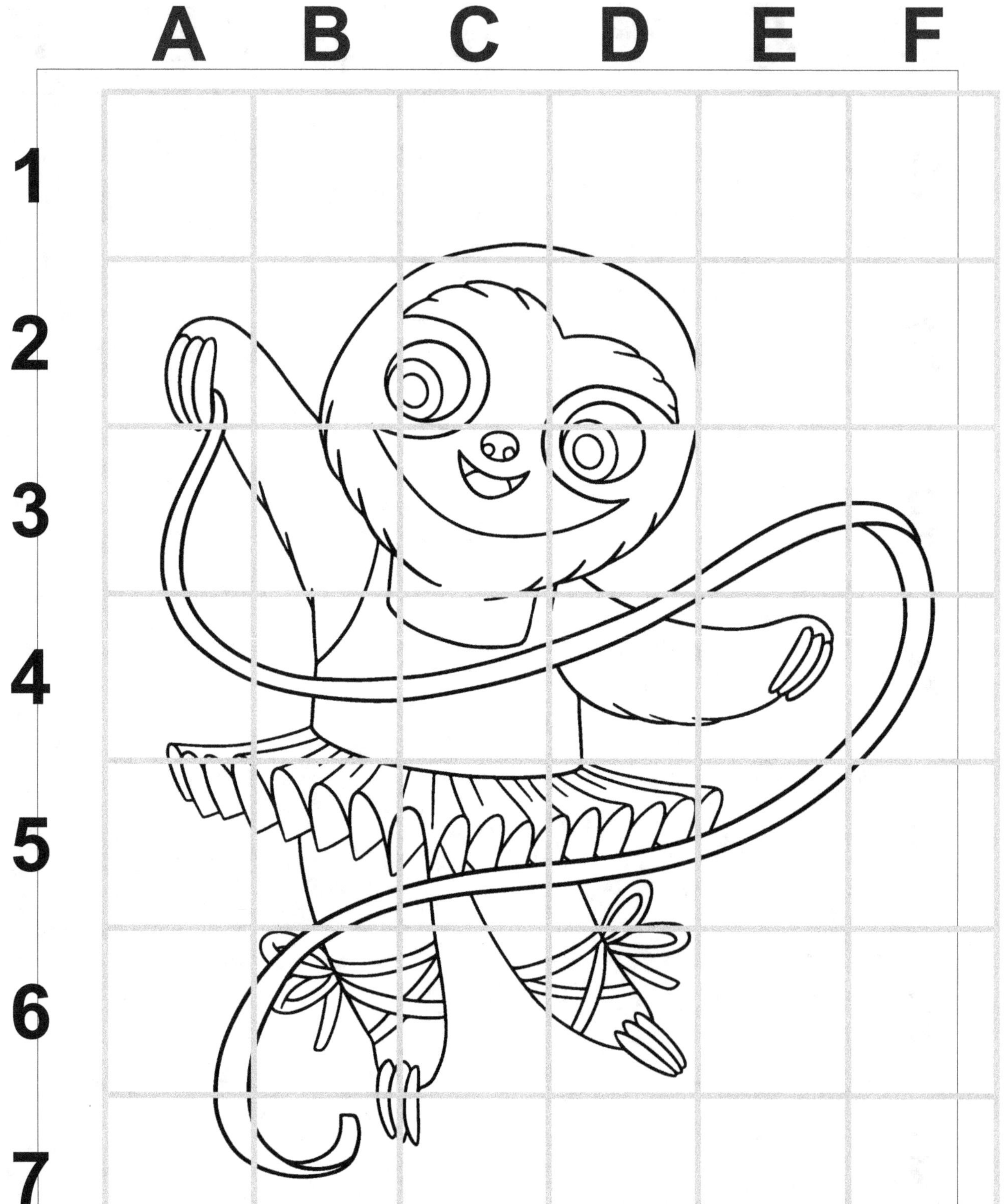
A
B
C
D
E
F
1
2
3
4
5
6
7

YOUR TURN

	A	B	C	D	E	F
1						
2						
3						
4						
5						
6						
7						

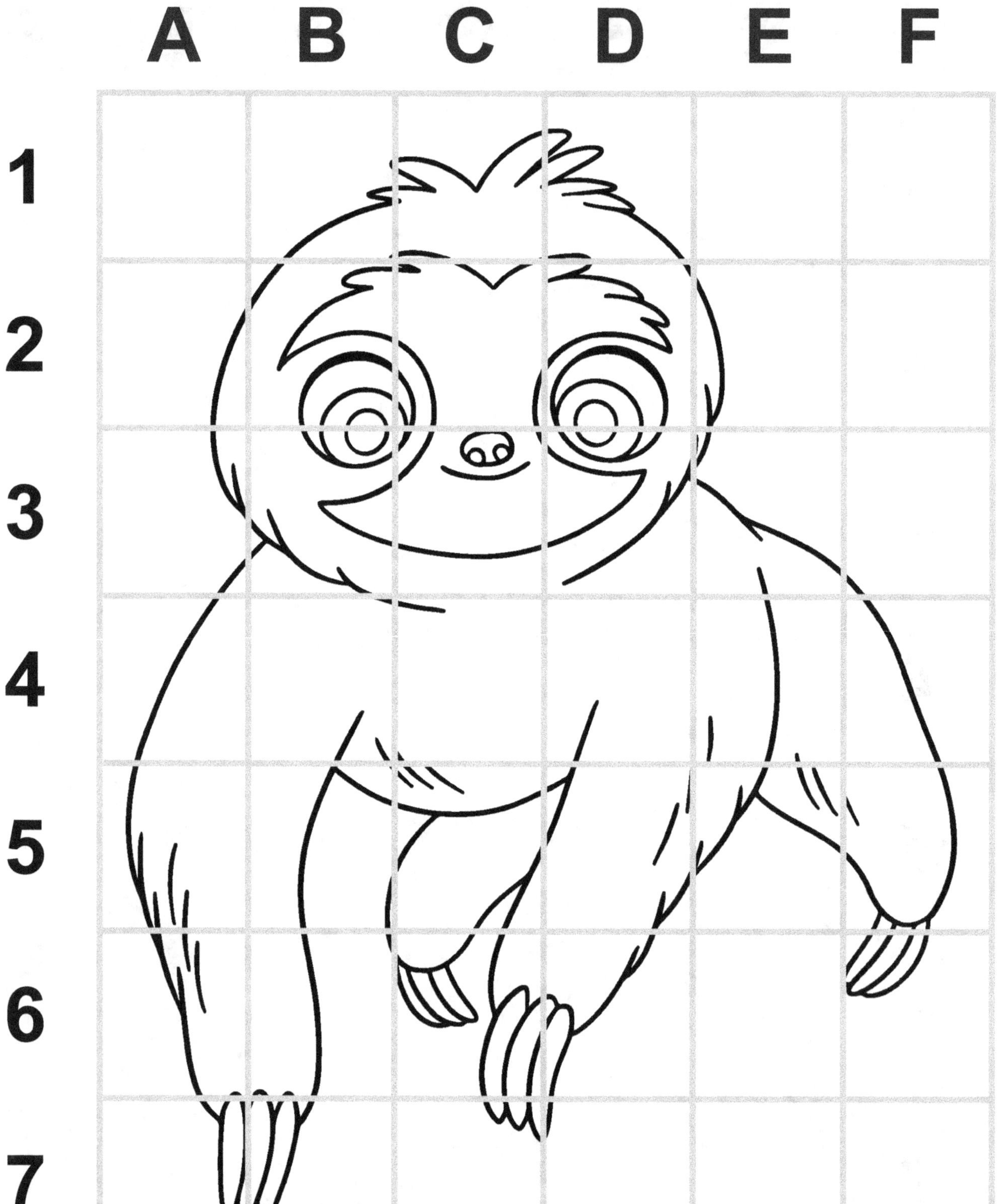
A B C D E F
1
2
3
4
5
6
7

YOUR TURN

	A	B	C	D	E	F
1						
2						
3						
4						
5						
6						
7						

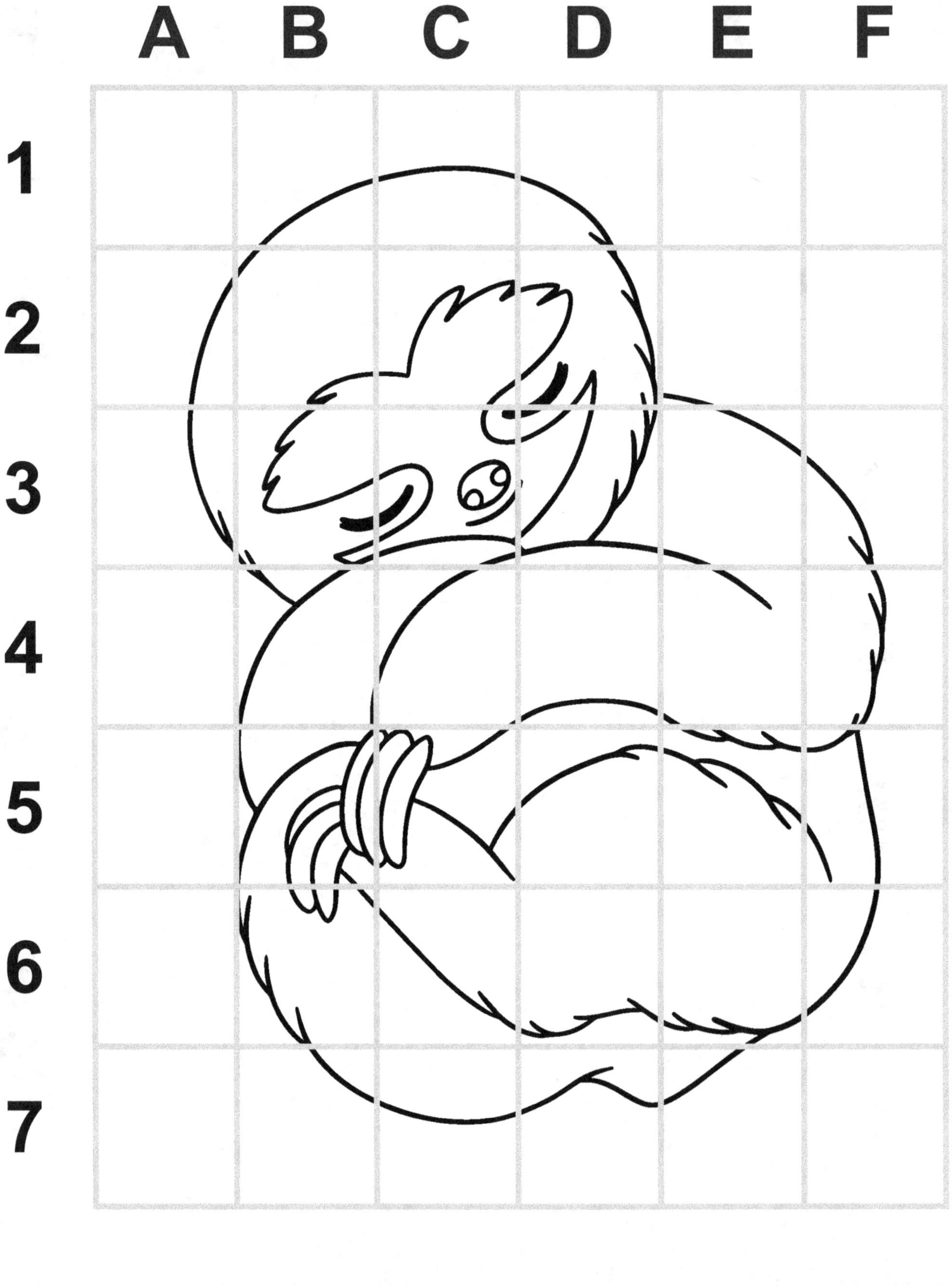
A
B
C
D
E
F
1
2
3
4
5
6
7

YOUR TURN

	A	B	C	D	E	F
1						
2						
3						
4						
5						
6						
7						

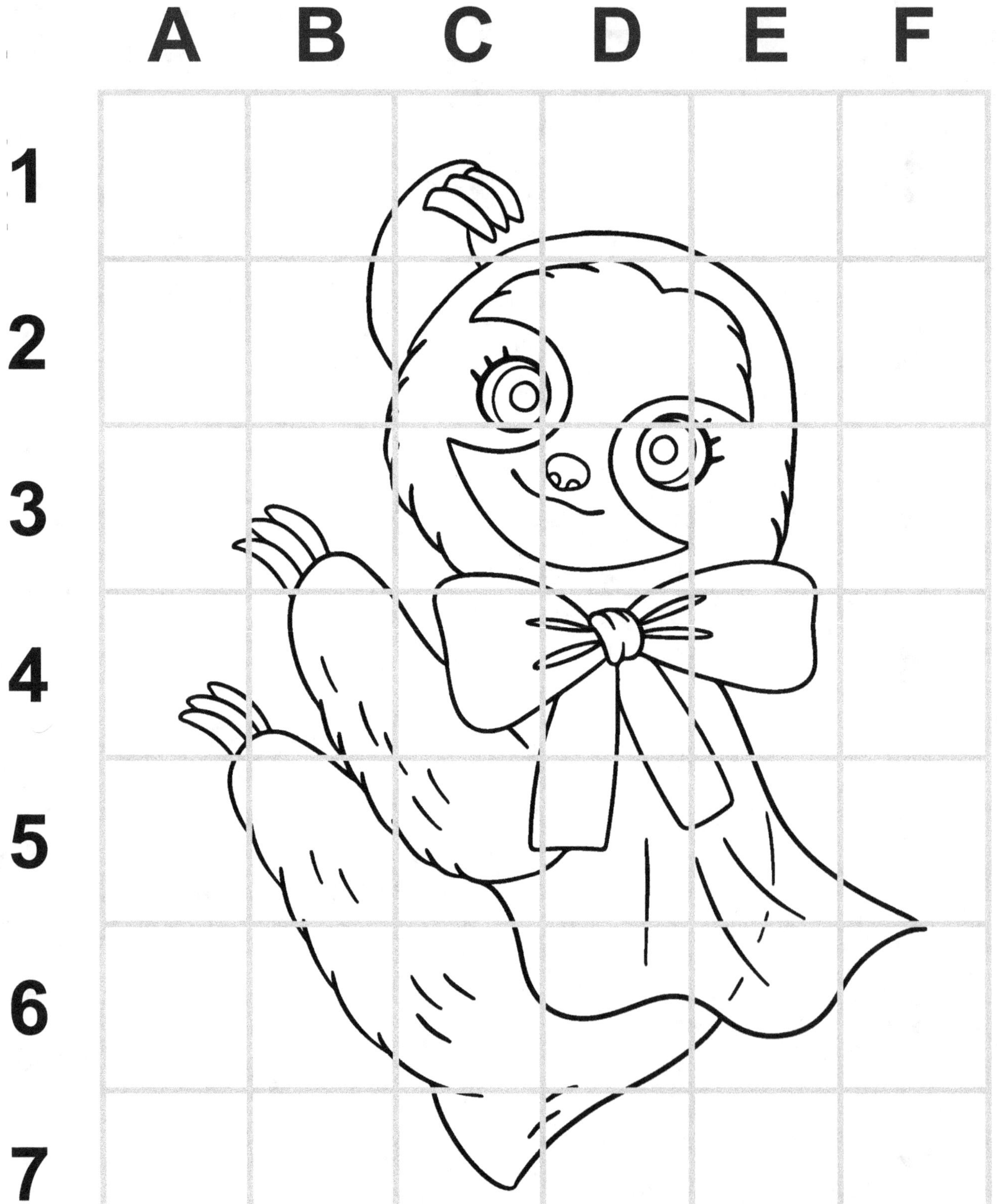
A B C D E F
1
2
3
4
5
6
7

YOUR TURN

	A	B	C	D	E	F
1						
2						
3						
4						
5						
6						
7						

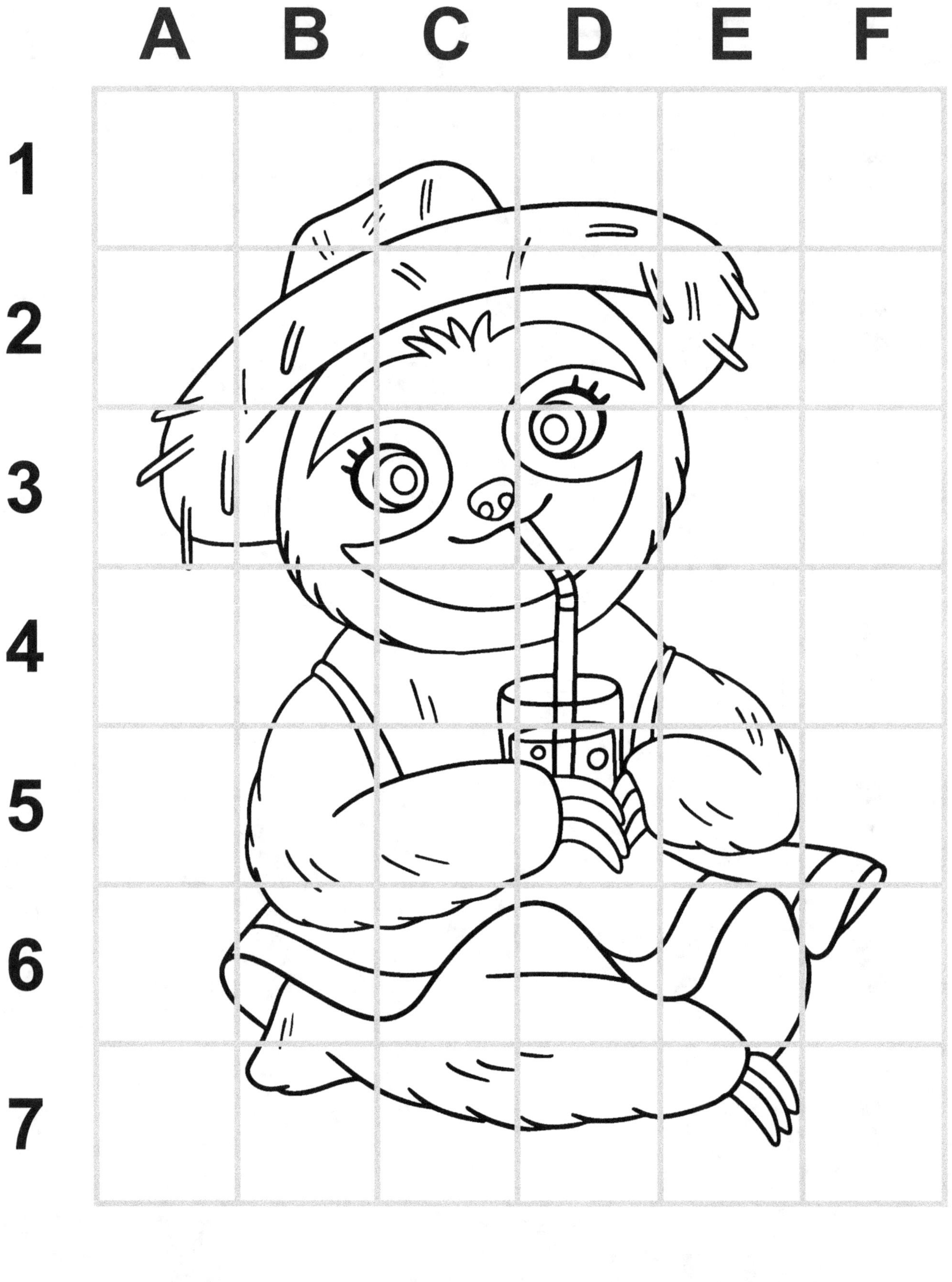
A B C D E F
1
2
3
4
5
6
7

YOUR TURN

	A	B	C	D	E	F
1						
2						
3						
4						
5						
6						
7						

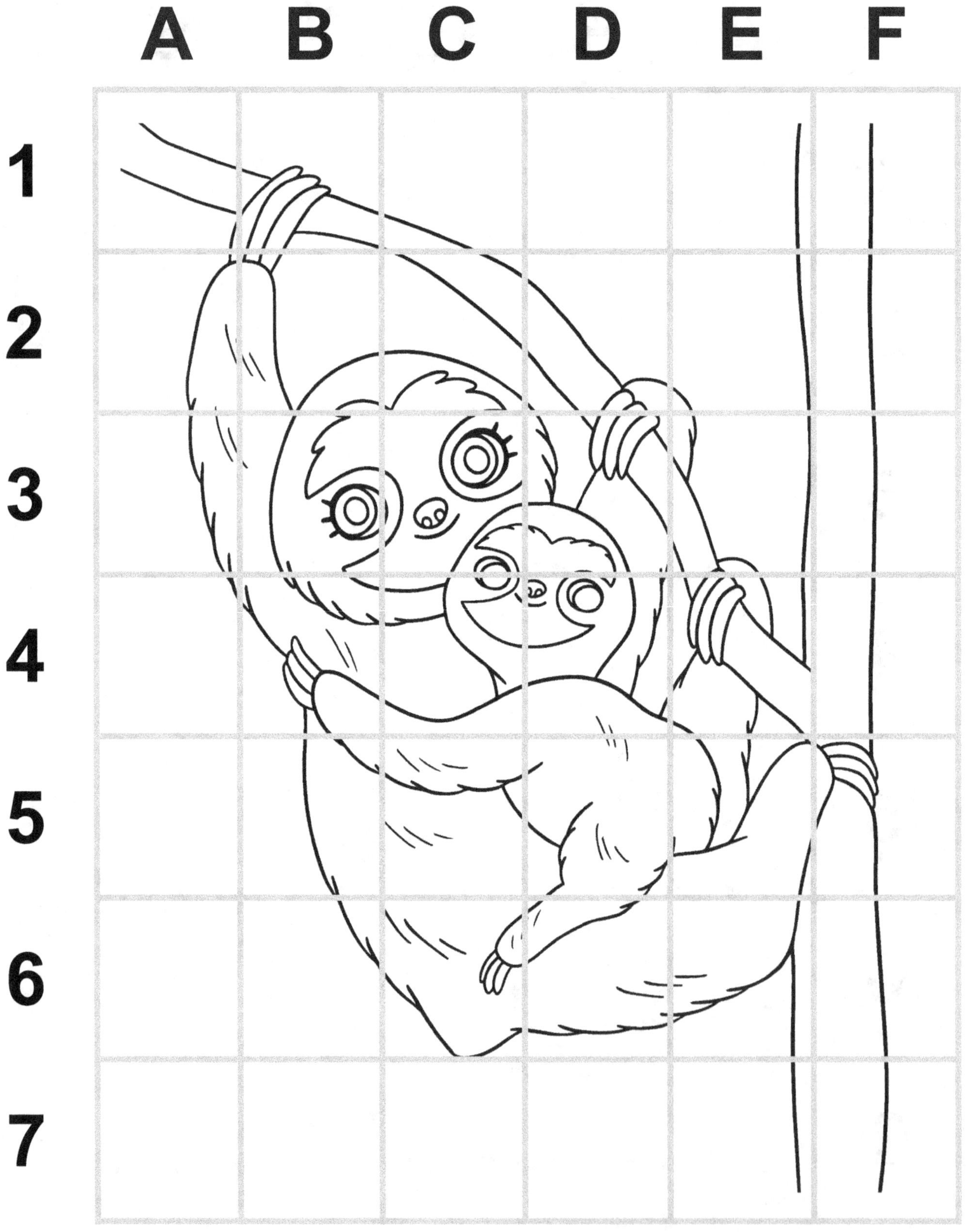
A B C D E F
1
2
3
4
5
6
7

YOUR TURN

	A	B	C	D	E	F
1						
2						
3						
4						
5						
6						
7						

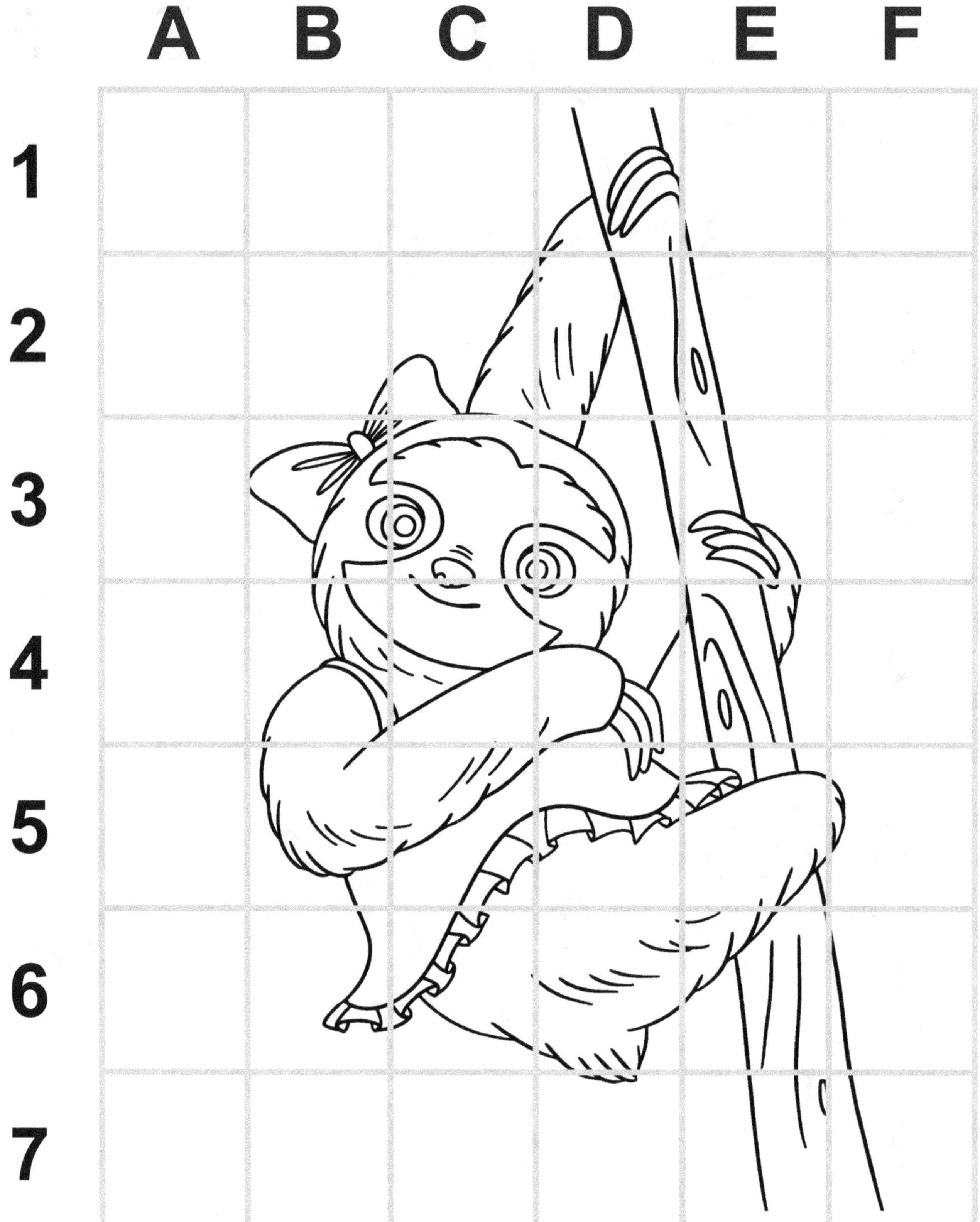
A B C D E F
1
2
3
4
5
6
7

YOUR TURN

	A	B	C	D	E	F
1						
2						
3						
4						
5						
6						
7						

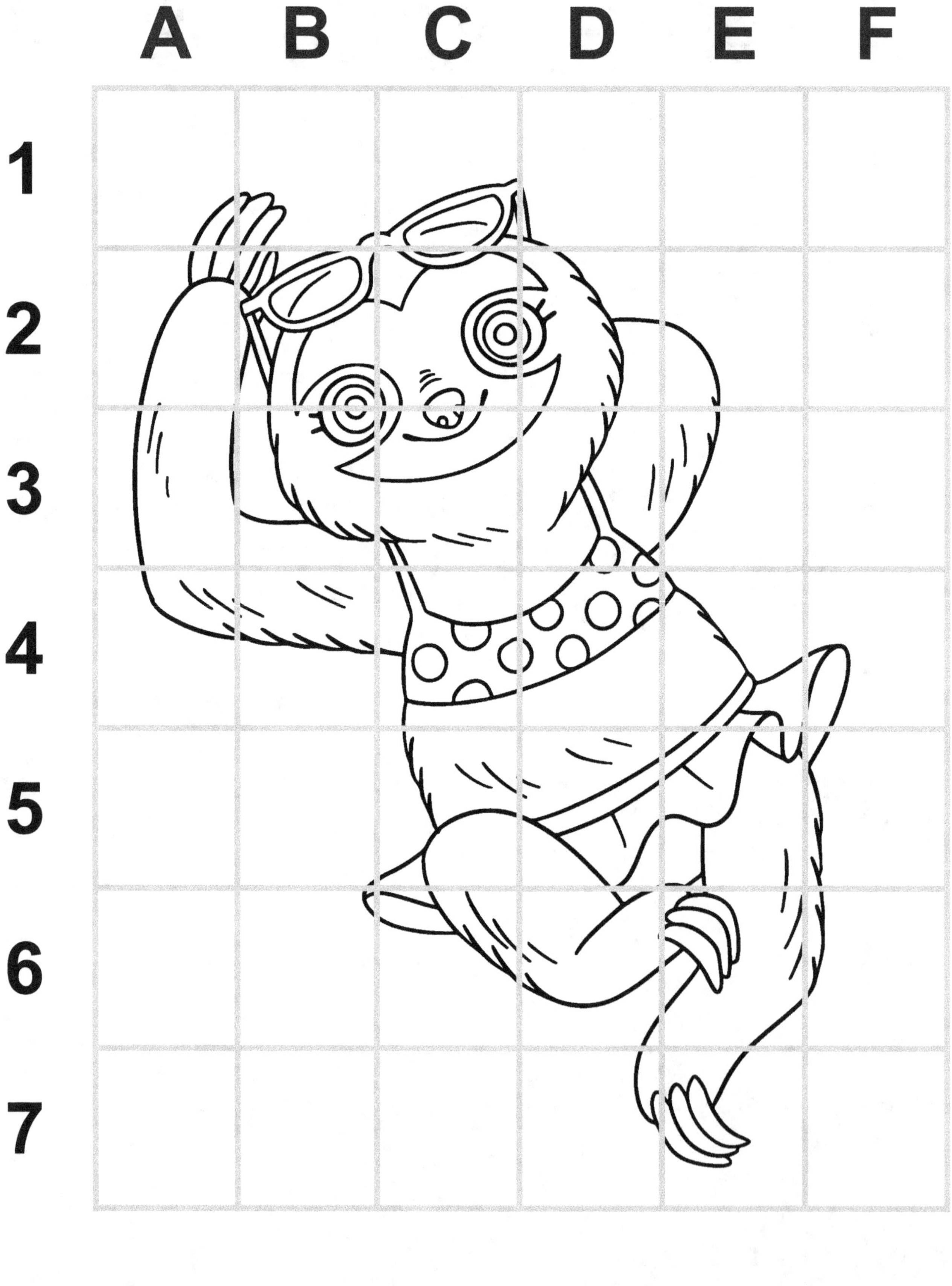
A
B
C
D
E
F
1
2
3
4
5
6
7

YOUR TURN

	A	B	C	D	E	F
1						
2						
3						
4						
5						
6						
7						

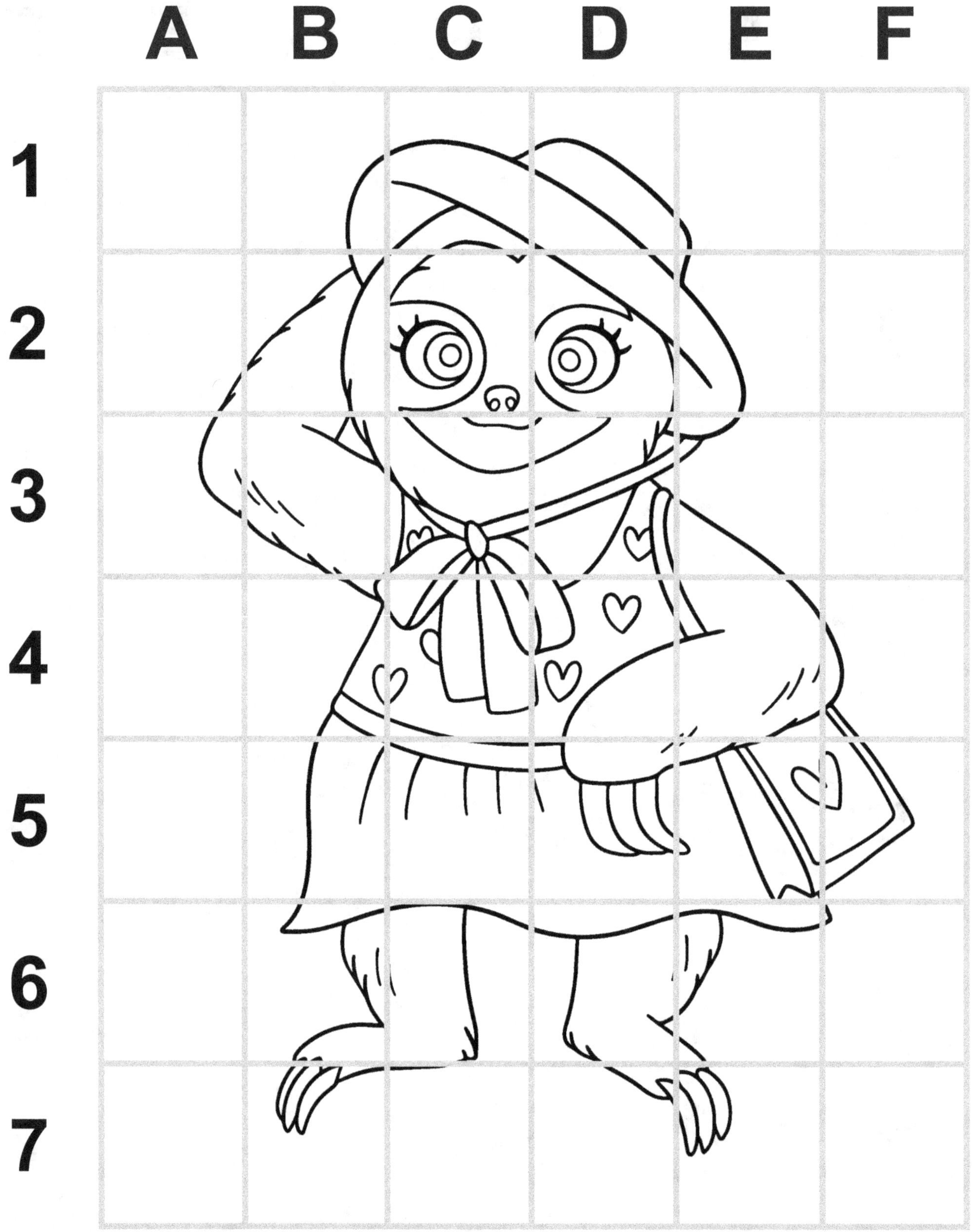
A B C D E F
1
2
3
4
5
6
7

YOUR TURN

	A	B	C	D	E	F
1						
2						
3						
4						
5						
6						
7						

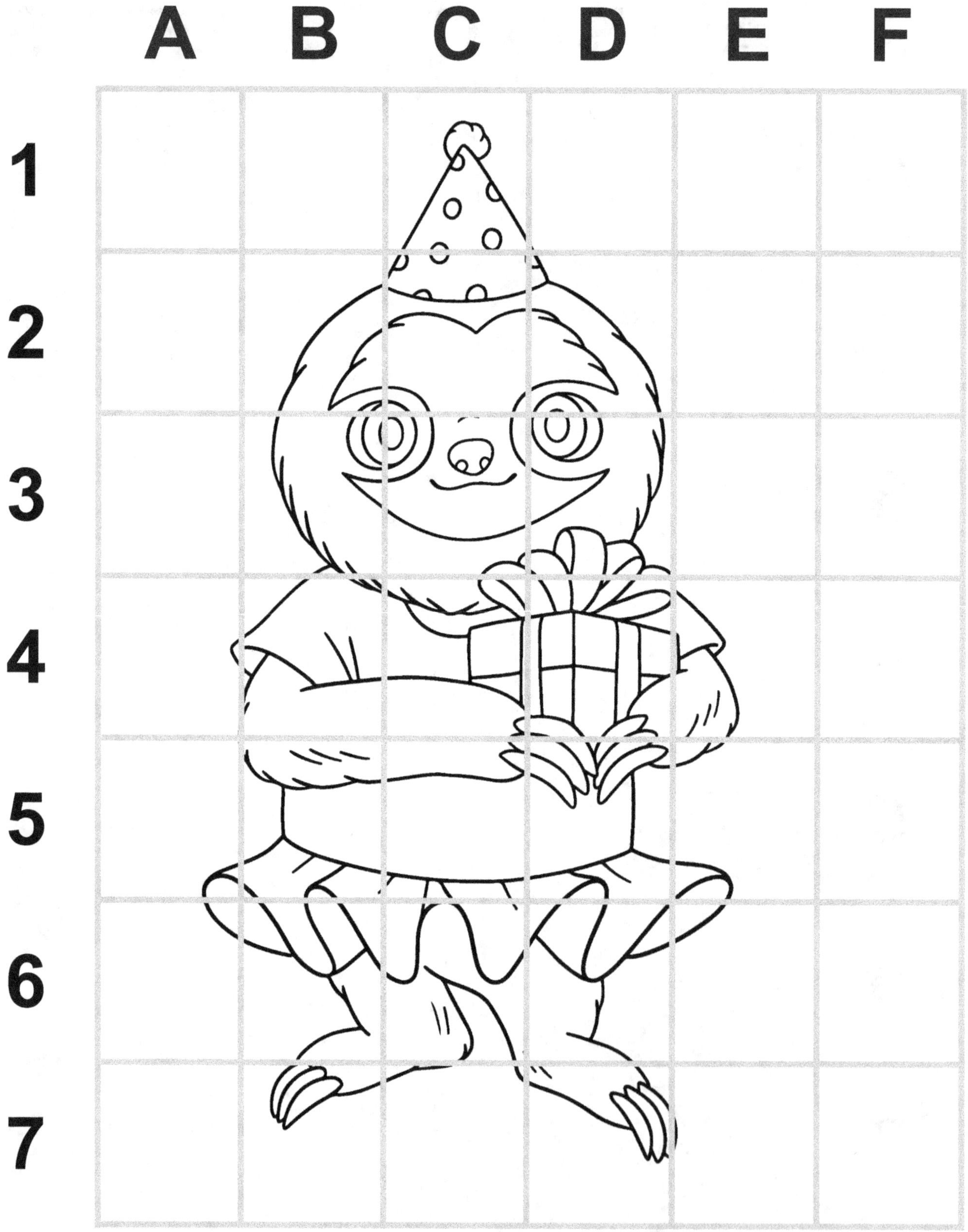
A B C D E F
1
2
3
4
5
6
7

YOUR TURN

	A	B	C	D	E	F
1						
2						
3						
4						
5						
6						
7						

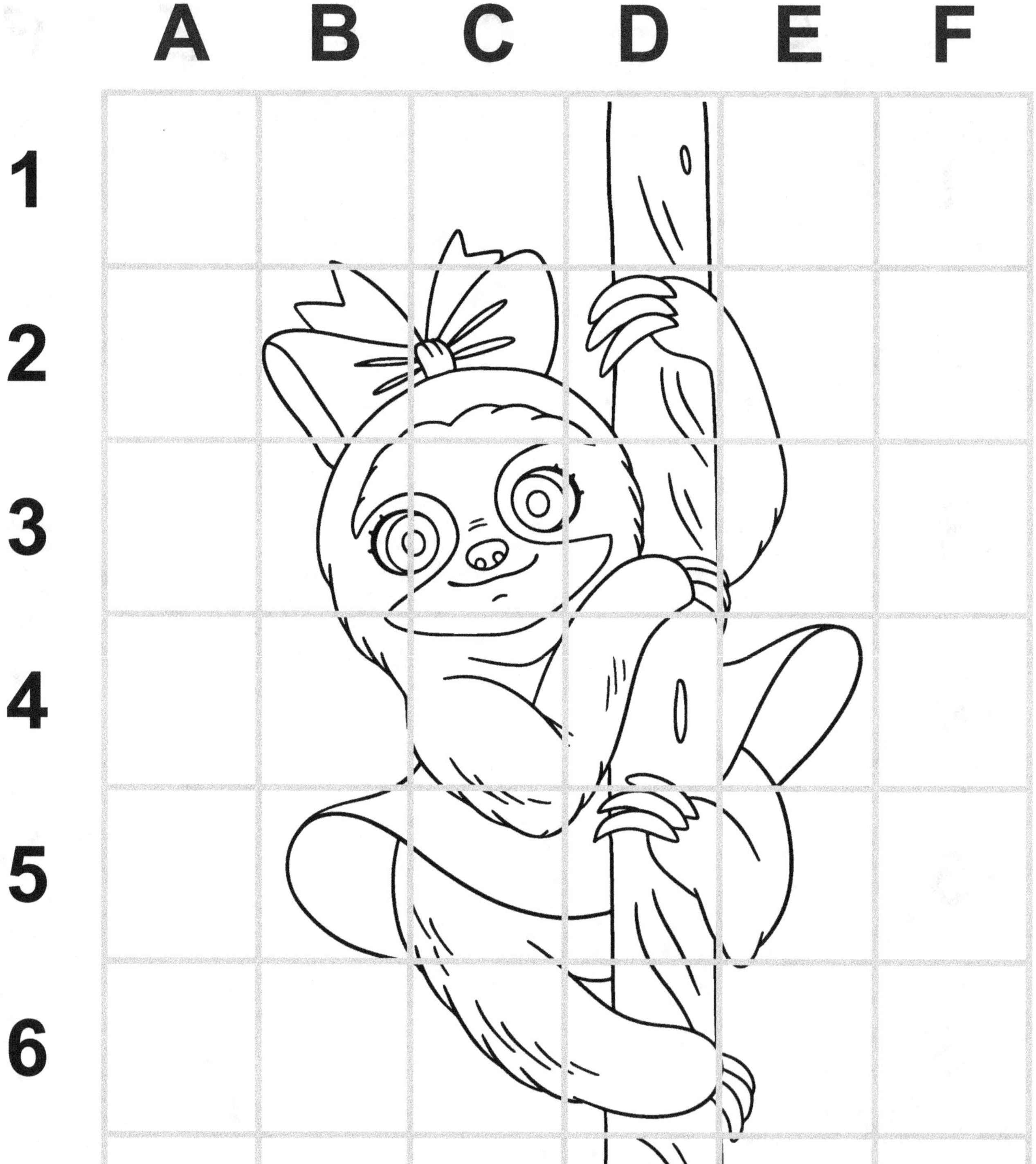
A B C D E F
1
2
3
4
5
6
7

YOUR TURN

	A	B	C	D	E	F
1						
2						
3						
4						
5						
6						
7						

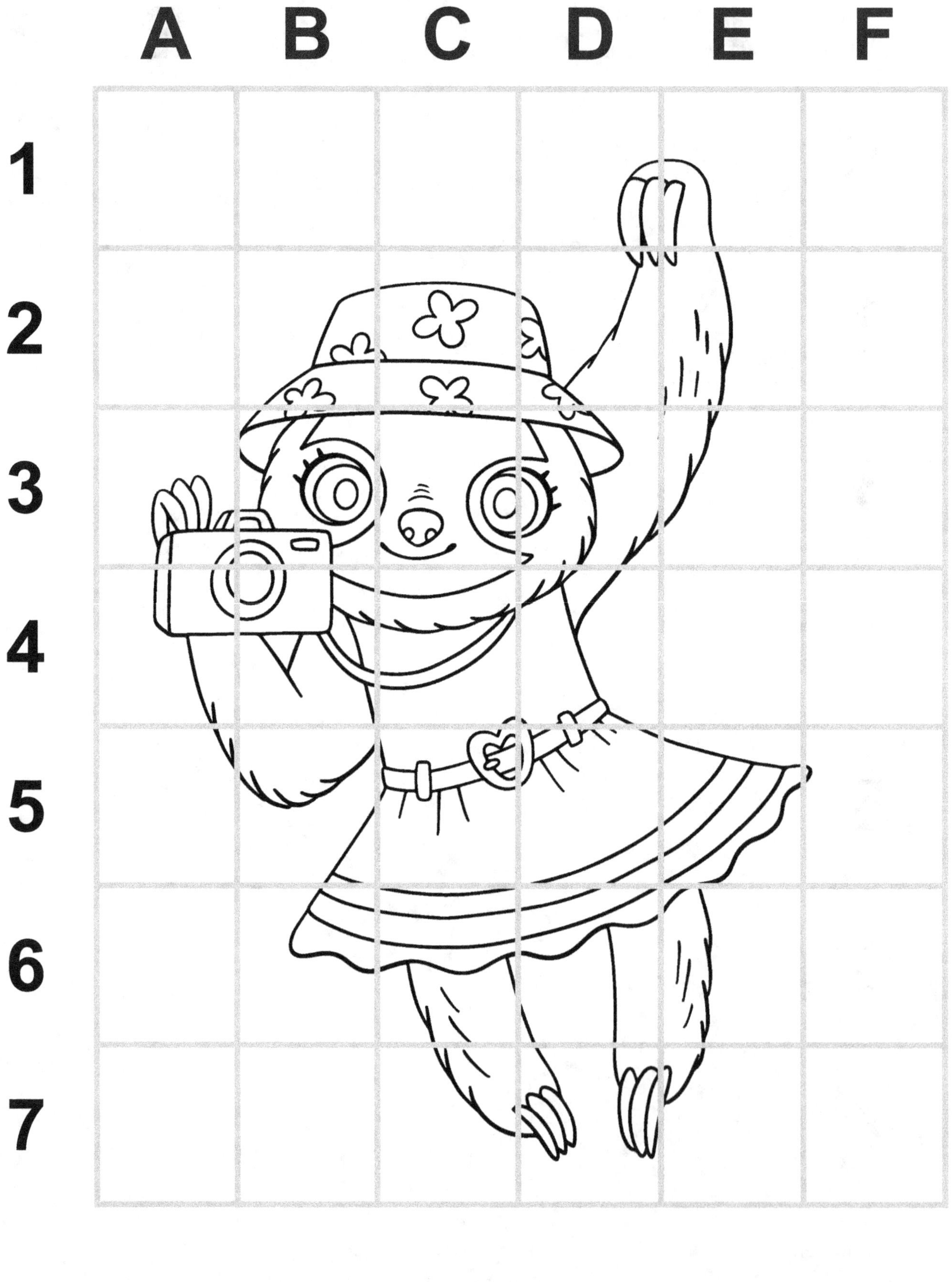
A B C D E F
1
2
3
4
5
6
7

YOUR TURN

	A	B	C	D	E	F
1						
2						
3						
4						
5						
6						
7						

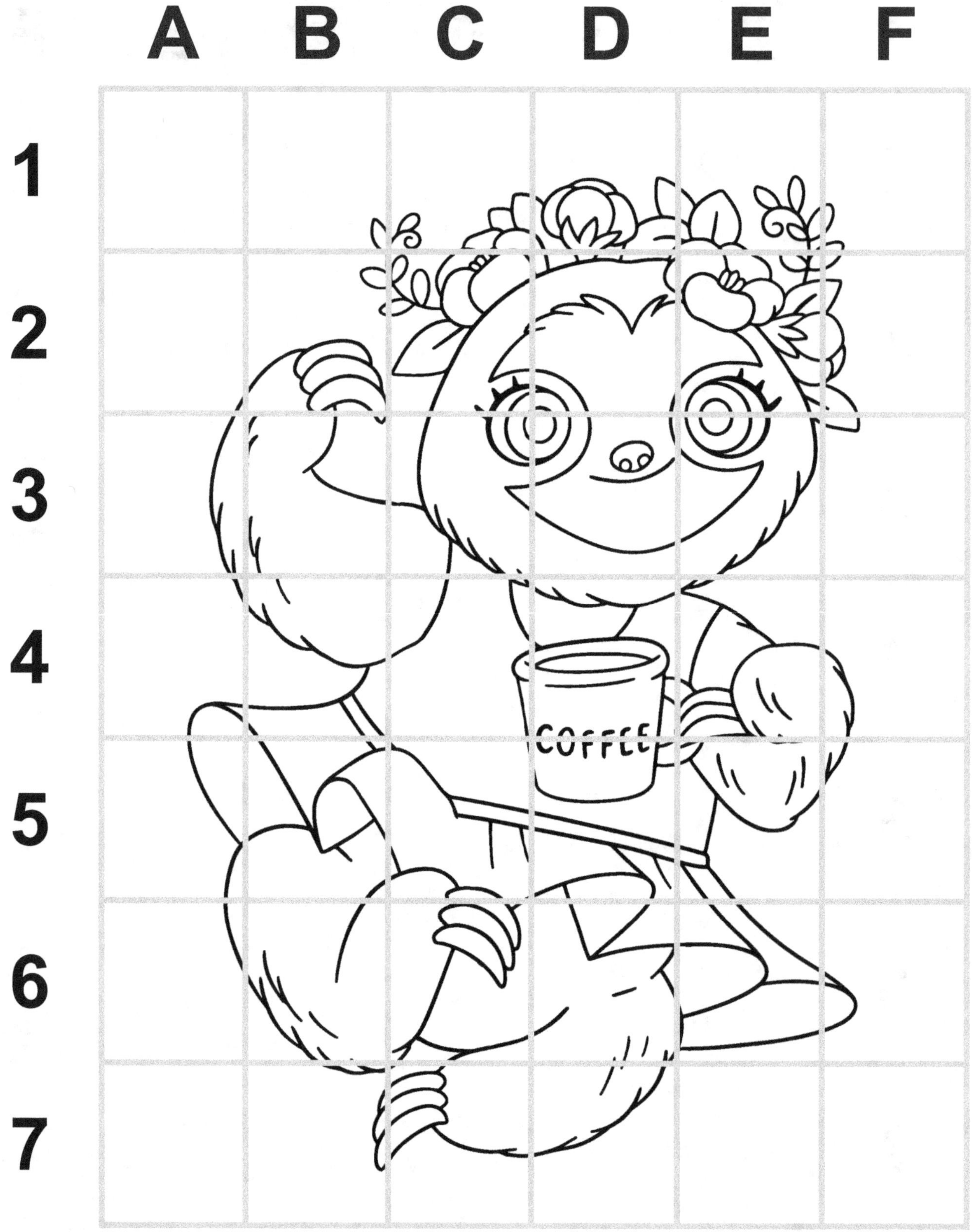
A B C D E F
1
2
3
4
5
6
7
COFFEE

Your turn

	A	B	C	D	E	F
1						
2						
3						
4						
5						
6						
7						

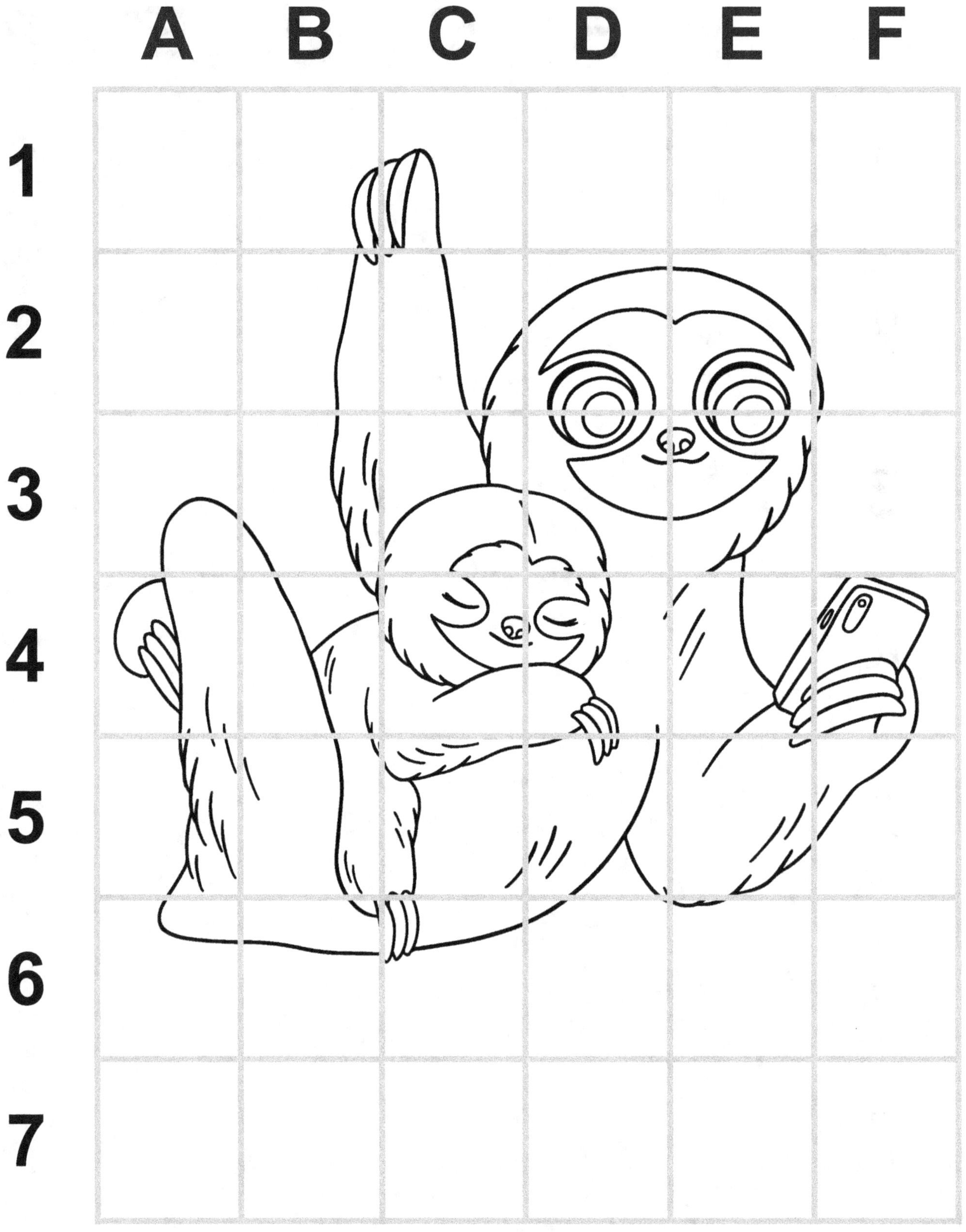
A B C D E F
1
2
3
4
5
6
7

YOUR TURN

	A	B	C	D	E	F
1						
2						
3						
4						
5						
6						
7						

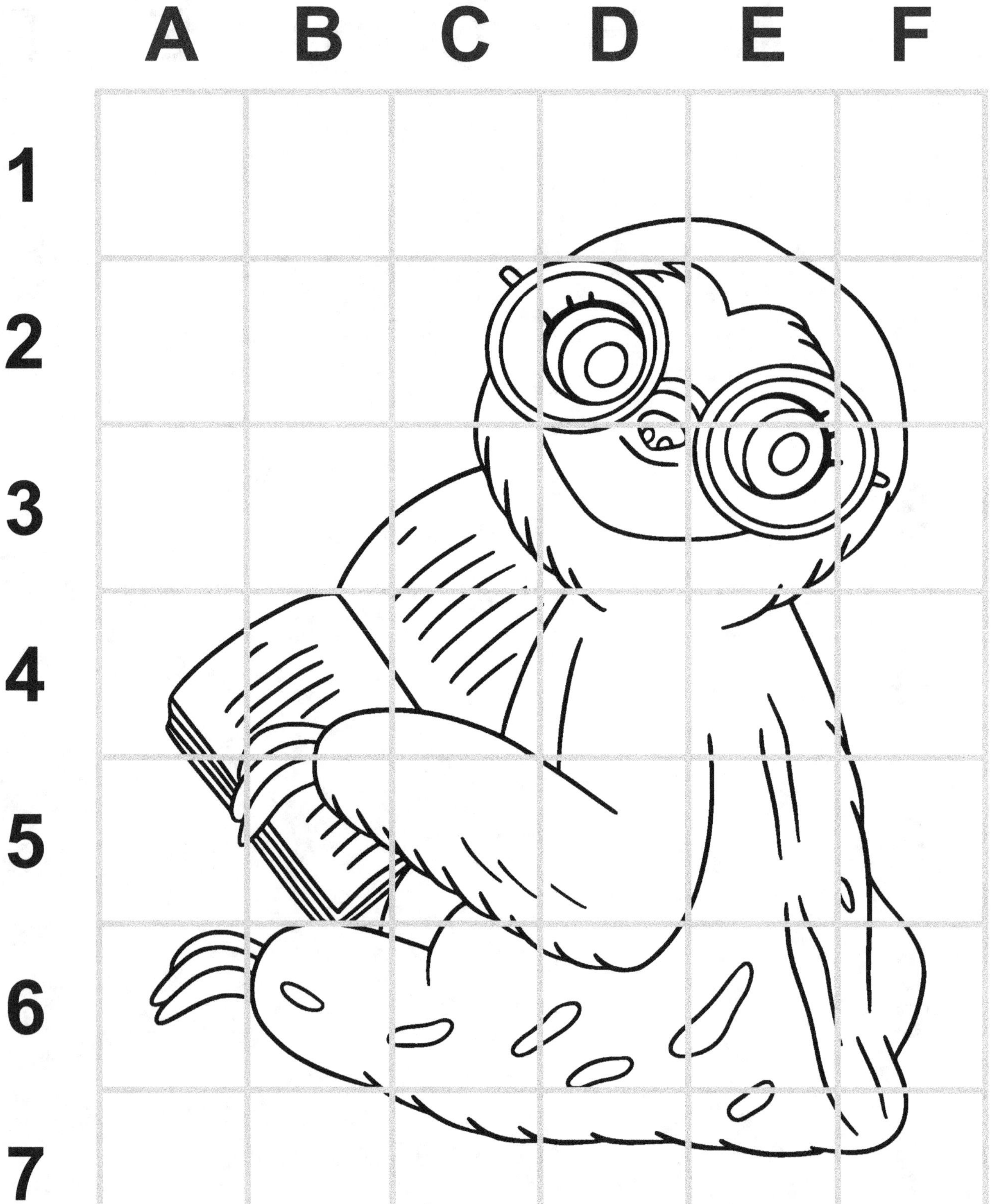
A B C D E F
1
2
3
4
5
6
7

YOUR TURN

	A	B	C	D	E	F
1						
2						
3						
4						
5						
6						
7						

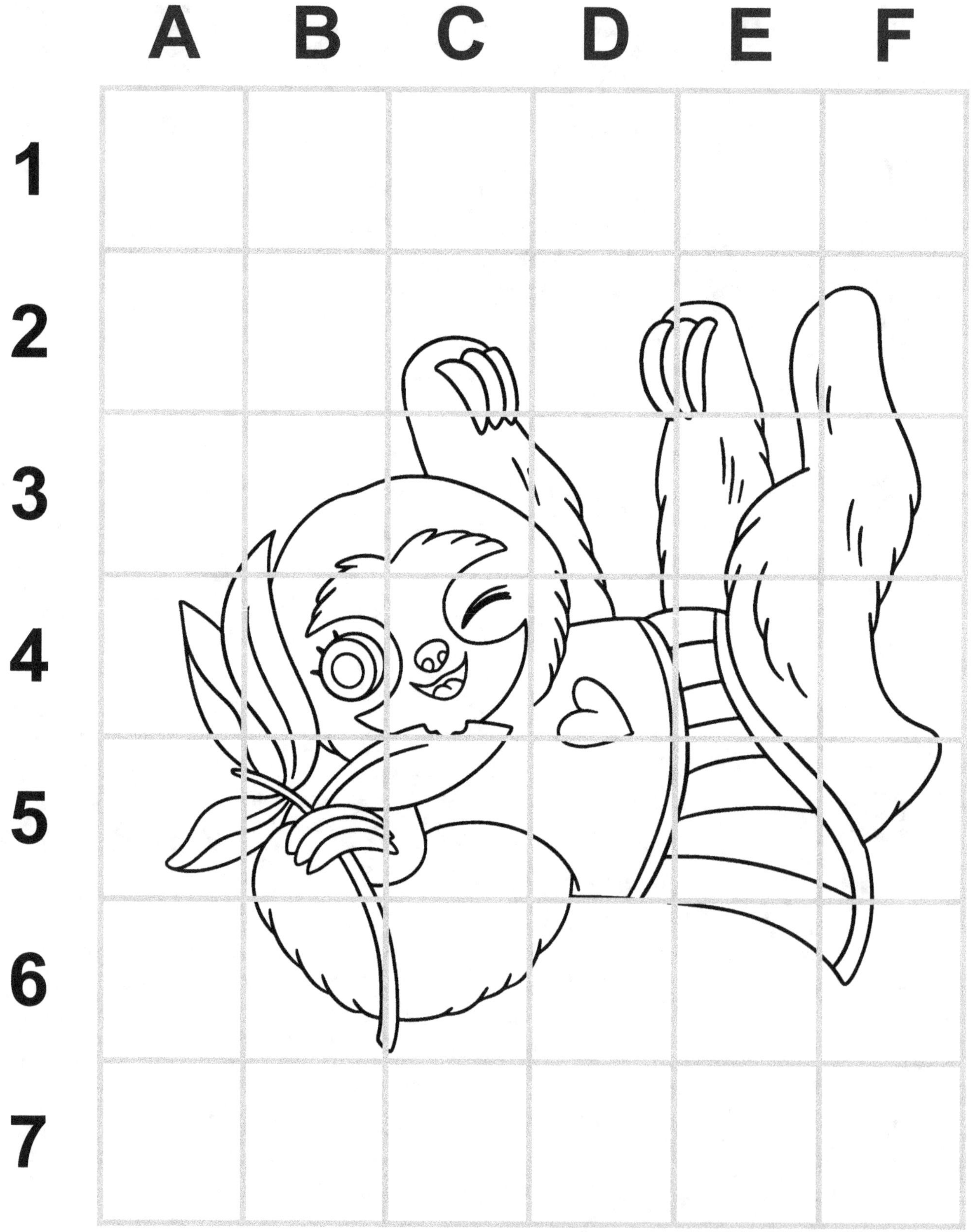
A B C D E F
1
2
3
4
5
6
7

YOUR TURN

	A	B	C	D	E	F
1						
2						
3						
4						
5						
6						
7						

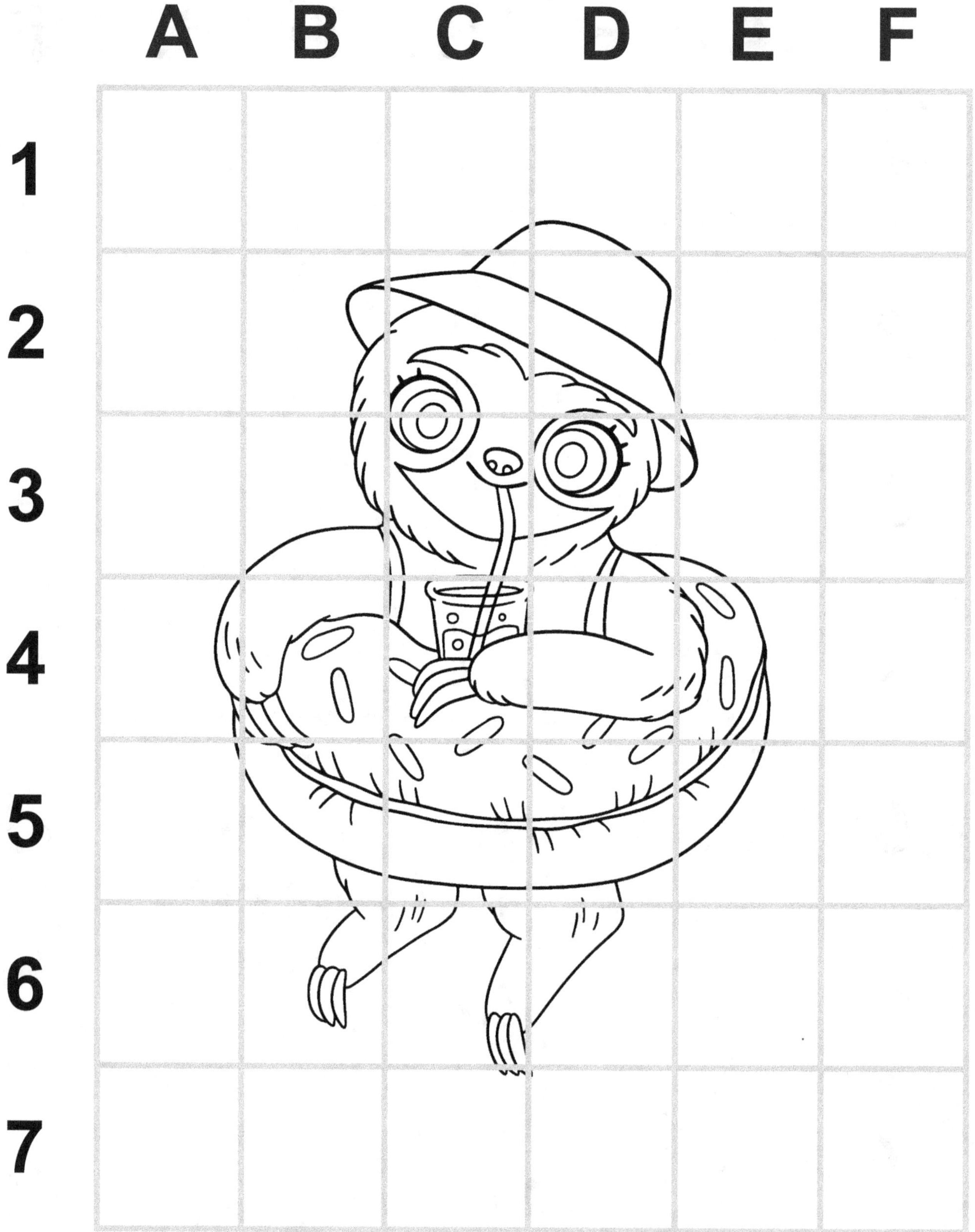
A
B
C
D
E
F
1
2
3
4
5
6
7

YOUR TURN

	A	B	C	D	E	F
1						
2						
3						
4						
5						
6						
7						

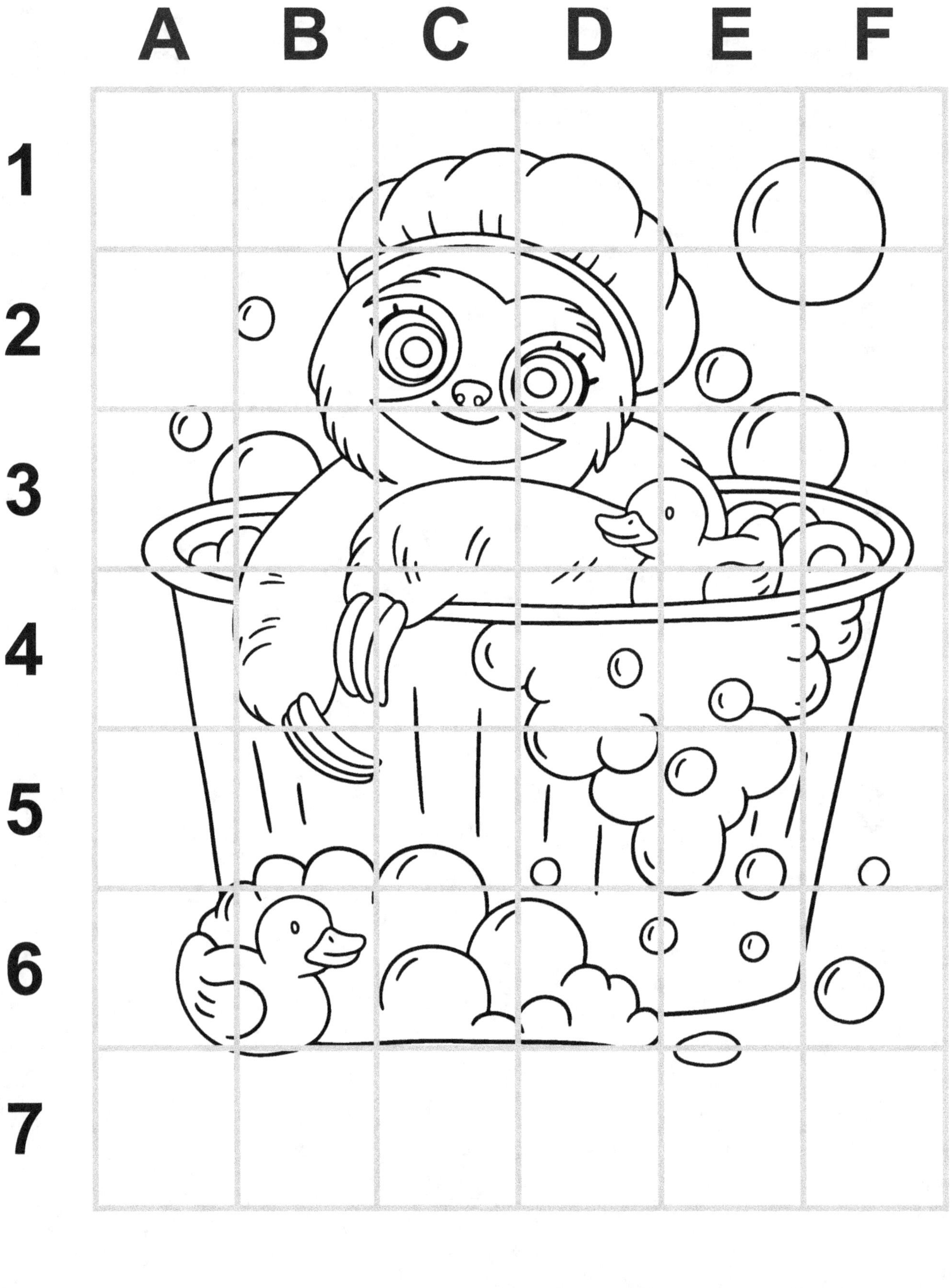
A B C D E F
1
2
3
4
5
6
7

YOUR TURN

	A	B	C	D	E	F
1						
2						
3						
4						
5						
6						
7						

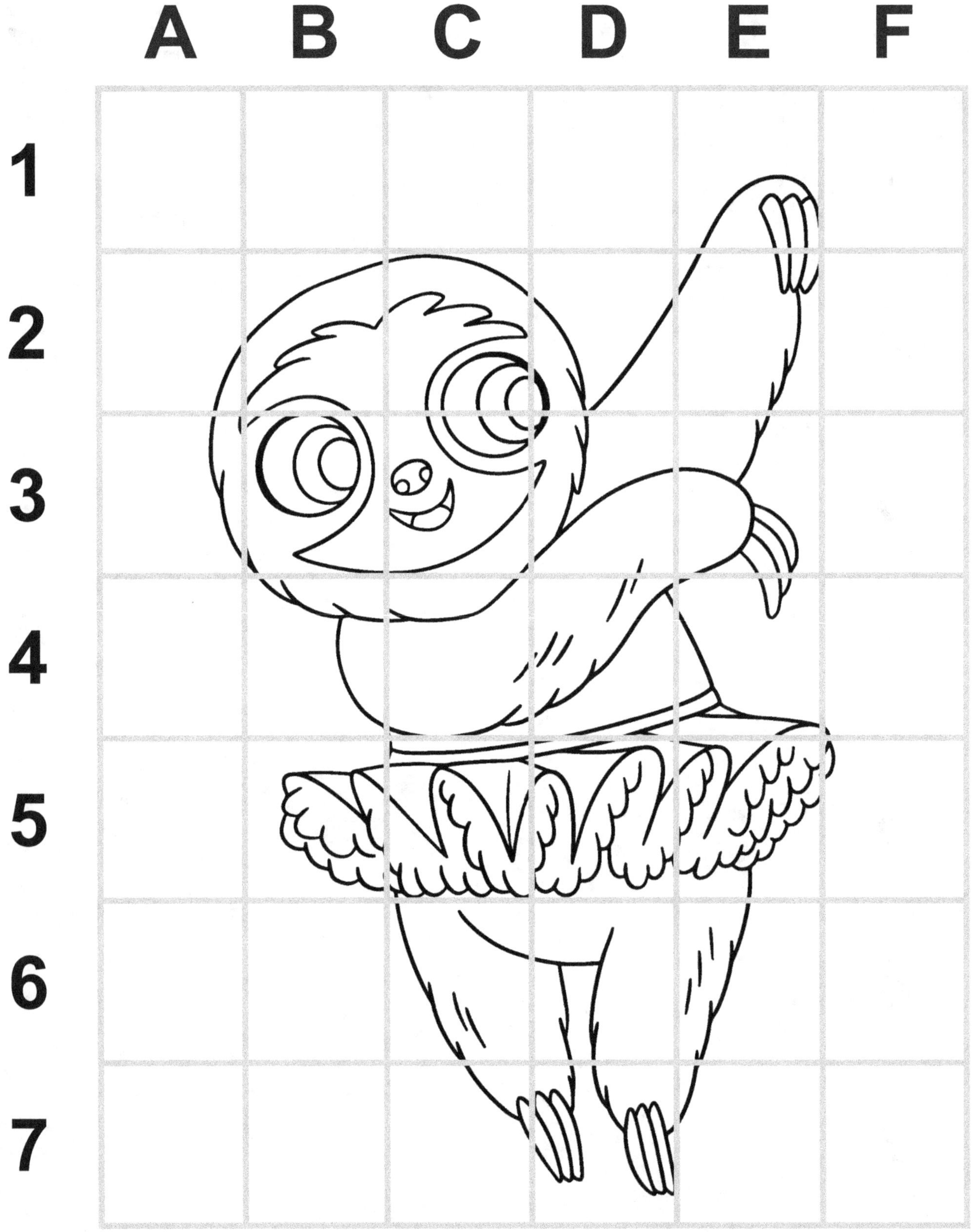
A B C D E F
1
2
3
4
5
6
7

YOUR TURN

	A	B	C	D	E	F
1						
2						
3						
4						
5						
6						
7						

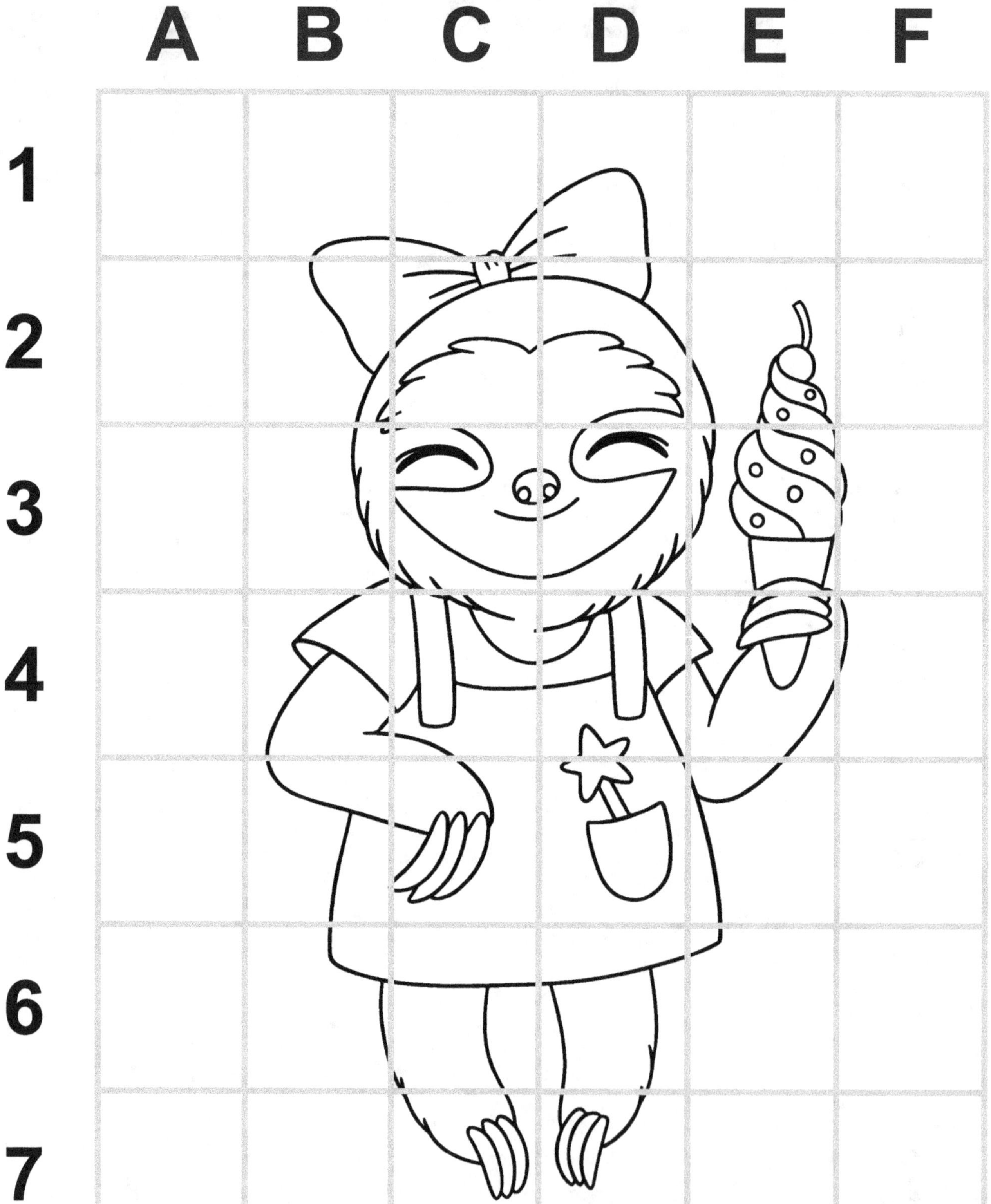
A B C D E F
1
2
3
4
5
6
7

YOUR TURN

	A	B	C	D	E	F
1						
2						
3						
4						
5						
6						
7						

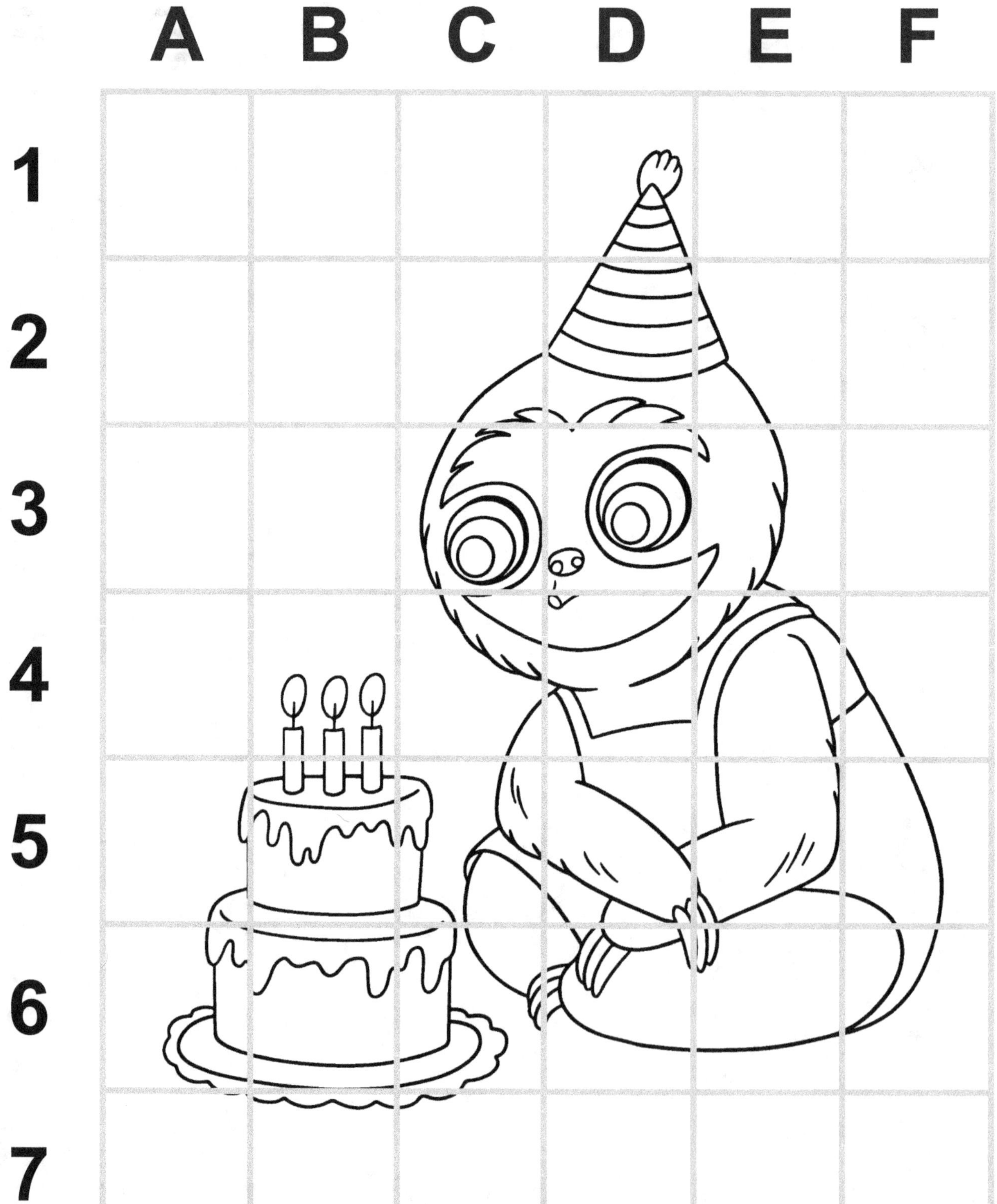
A B C D E F
1
2
3
4
5
6
7

YOUR TURN

	A	B	C	D	E	F
1						
2						
3						
4						
5						
6						
7						

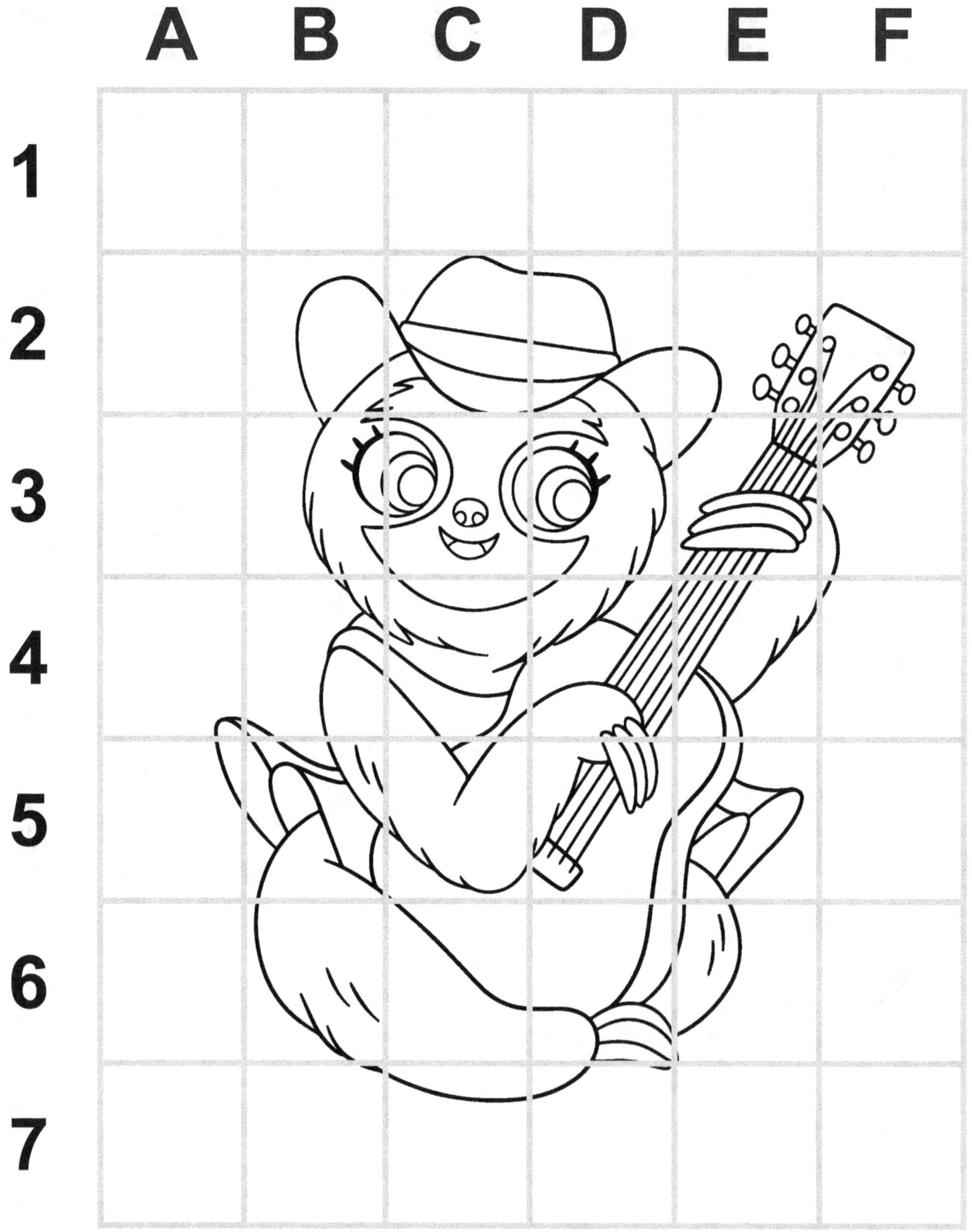
A B C D E F
1
2
3
4
5
6
7

YOUR TURN

	A	B	C	D	E	F
1						
2						
3						
4						
5						
6						
7						

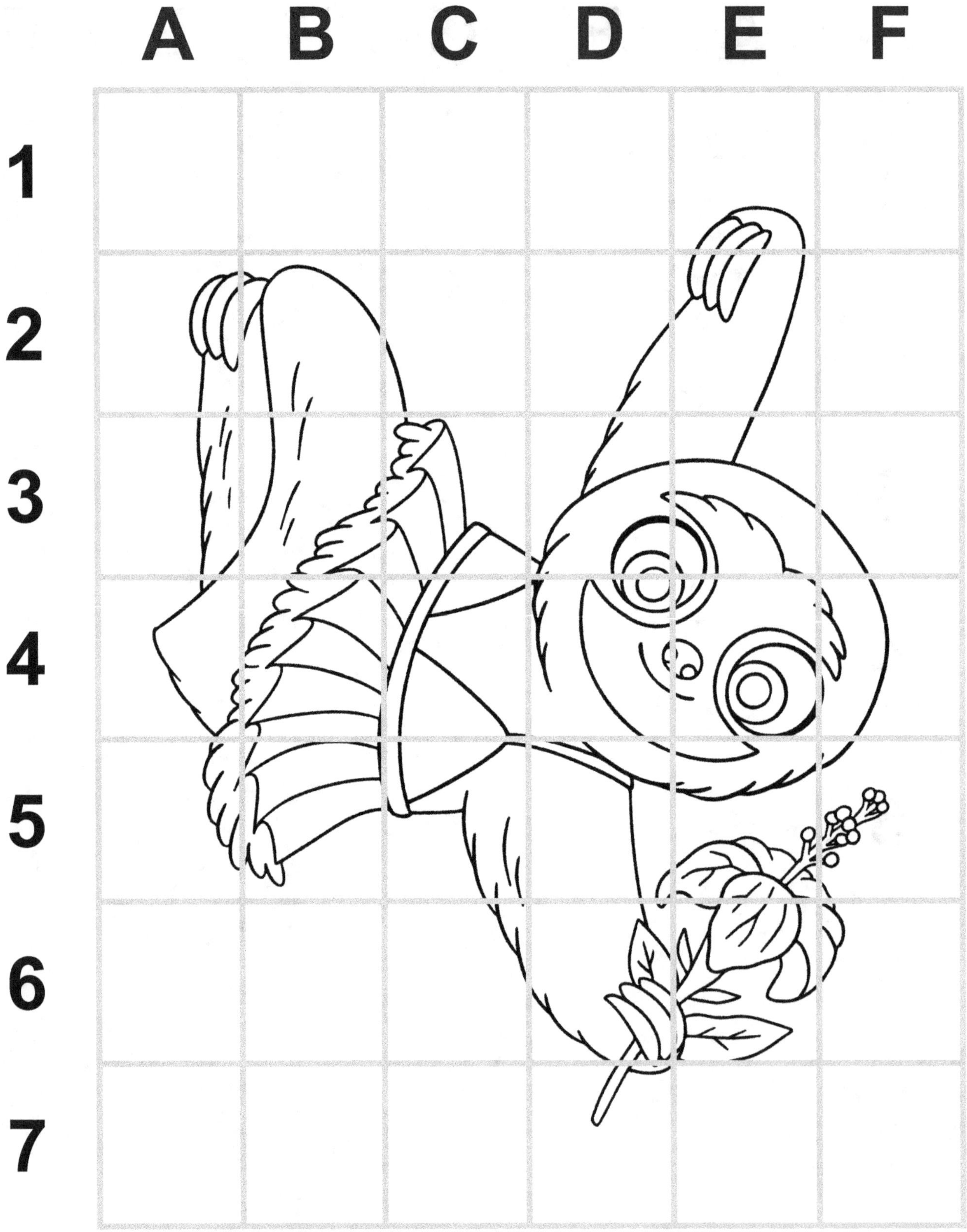
A B C D E F
1
2
3
4
5
6
7

YOUR TURN

	A	B	C	D	E	F
1						
2						
3						
4						
5						
6						
7						

www.ingramcontent.com/pod-product-compliance
Lightning Source LLC
Chambersburg PA
CBHW081539220526
45467CB00010B/3253
* 9 7 9 8 6 8 7 1 4 8 9 5 5 *